LIST

T0125455

SELECTED WORKS BY JAMES LAXER

Staking Claims to a Continent: John A. Macdonald, Abraham Lincoln, Jefferson Davis, and the Making of North America

Tecumseh & Brock: The War of 1812

Beyond the Bubble: Imagining a New Canàdian Economy

The Perils of Empire

Mission of Folly: Canada and Afghanistan

The Acadians: In Search of a Homeland

The Border: Canada, U.S. and Dispatches from the 49th Parallel

Stalking the Elephant: My Discovery of America
(U.S. Edition: Discovering America: Travels in the Land of Guns, God, and Corporate Gurus)

The Undeclared War: Class Conflict in the Age of Cyber Capitalism

In Search of a New Left:
Canadian Politics after the Neoconservative Assault

False God: How the Globalization Myth Has Impoverished Canada

Inventing Europe: The Rise of a New World Power

SELECTED WORKS FOR YOUNG READERS

Empire: A Groundwood Guide

Oil: A Groundwood Guide

Democracy: A Groundwood Guide

Tecumseh

RED DIAPER BABY

A BOYHOOD IN THE AGE OF McCARTHYISM

JAMES LAXER

First published in 2004 by Douglas & McIntyre Ltd.
This edition published in Canada in 2019 and the USA in 2019 by
House of Anansi Press Inc.
www.houseofanansi.com

House of Anansi Press is committed to protecting our natural environment.
As part of our efforts, the interior of this book is printed on paper that contains
100% post-consumer recycled fibres, is acid-free, and is processed chlorine-free.

23 22 21 20 19   1 2 3 4 5

Library and Archives Canada Cataloguing in Publication

Laxer, James, author
Red diaper baby : a boyhood in the age of McCarthyism
/ James Laxer.

Originally published: Vancouver: Douglas & McIntyre, 2004.
Issued in print and electronic formats.
ISBN 978-1-4870-0676-1 (softcover).—ISBN 978-1-4870-0677-8
(EPUB).—ISBN 978-1-4870-0678-5 (Kindle)

Laxer, James—Childhood and youth. 2. Communism—
Ontario—Toronto—History. 3. Toronto (Ont.)—Biography.
4. Biographies. I. Title.

FC601.L39A3 2019   335.43092   C2018-906100-6
C2018-906101-4

Library of Congress Control Number: 2018962470

Series design: Brian Morgan
Cover illustration: Patrick Gray
Text design and typesetting: Sara Loos

*We acknowledge for their financial support of our publishing program the Canada
Council for the Arts, the Ontario Arts Council, and the Government of Canada.*

Printed and bound in Canada

To Gord and Linda

Introduction by Mel Watkins

The present year, 2019, is the fiftieth anniversary of the publication of the *Waffle Manifesto for an Independent Socialist Canada* — a mouthful indeed, and a product of that most exciting of decades, the 1960s. The idea for it, and for its proclamation by a left caucus within the NDP, came from the late Jim Laxer, which makes this an opportune time to reissue a fascinating book by him about his childhood.

As an adult, Jim wrote more than twenty books, but this one, *Red Diaper Baby*, is arguably his best — full of personal feelings, political insight, and very good writing. I liked it when I first read it. I like it just as much rereading it, and it certainly merits rediscovery. The original was the winner of the Canadian Jewish Book Award for the best biography/memoir in 2005.

The title is a phrase commonly applied to the children of Communists, and Jim's childhood was not one of your average, ordinary kind — like mine, for example, rural and deeply conservative. His parents were indeed members of the Communist Party, his father a full-time organizer. The Party was outlawed in 1940, then known after the Second World War as the Labour-Progressive Party and linked to the Soviet Union. Jim was born in 1941 — missing Stalin's birthday by just a few days and saving his being named Joseph — during the Second World War, when Canada and the Soviet Union were on the same side, opposing Nazi Germany. But after the hot war came the Cold War, with Canada and the Soviet Union on opposing sides, and with the Cold War came McCarthyism in the United States, demonizing Communism and its practitioners.

Children like Jim were lied to and learned how to lie, to lead a secret life, to be true believers. Interestingly, he was the descendant of true believers of a different kind: his paternal grandfather a rabbi, his maternal grandfather a Protestant missionary and minister. His mother told his school that his father was a freelance journalist. Looking back on it, Jim writes, "the Communist world view was coherent, and it had answers for the great questions of life and existence. I was open to it. I imbibed it, breathed it in and accepted it."

The biggest lie was about the nature of the Soviet Union and of its murderous leader Joseph Stalin. When Stalin died in 1953, Jim's father told him "it is a great tragedy that Stalin will not be able to finish his work."

You may not think such a childhood would produce a leading advocate of democracy within the NDP and Canada, but that is what actually happened in Jim's case. Read this book and learn how that came to pass with the implosion of Stalinism in the mid-1950s, when its sins — and they were serious — were exposed by Khrushchev, and Hungary was invaded by the Soviet Union in 1956. In 1957, Jim's parents left the Party and Jim felt liberated, a Canadian like the others — which may help to explain how he became an iconic Canadian nationalist.

This is a memoir about the political, but it is also about the personal. You don't have to be on the left — though you should be! — to enjoy this book. You will get to know Jim, a very funny person with a marvellous sense of the absurd. Perhaps that is how he coped with the crudities of Communism, though he was helped greatly, I know, by being part of a loving family.

In the fullness of time, Jim became both gutsy and prescient, two essential qualities for doing good politics. And throughout his life that was to be his focus, until his death in 2018, at age seventy-six.

I leave it to you, the reader, to decide how Jim's childhood link to the Communist Party underlay his impressive achievements as a public intellectual on the Canadian left. My guess would be that his deep and imaginative and lifelong interest in politics was part of his DNA as a Red Diaper Baby, leading him to become devoted to the radicalization of the NDP as a democratic socialist party and to find his voice in the writing of Canadian history.

We owe it to ourselves in a time of absolutism and false gods and fake news to learn from this chronicle, which conveys a very special sense of how the Cold War was experienced by a Canadian child caught in its tangle.

MEL WATKINS is Professor Emeritus of Economics and Political Science at the University of Toronto. He is Editor Emeritus of *This Magazine* and a contributor to *Peace* magazine and Rabble.ca. Watkins was the recipient of the inaugural Galbraith Prize in Economics and Social Justice awarded by the Progressive Economics Forum in 2008. He founded the Waffle faction of the New Democratic Party with James Laxer in 1969.

Contents

Prologue

IN ONE OF MY PHOTO albums, I have a black-and-white picture of myself taken when I was two. The photo shows me looking perplexed and not a little sad. In it, I am holding a book called *Poland*, with a map of Europe on the cover. Poland is highlighted in the centre, with Nazi Germany and Soviet Russia looming menacingly on either side. Not typical reading matter for a two-year-old.

In the original version of the photo, I am sitting on my mother's lap. But decades ago, I cut out a portion of it, so that in my album it looks as if I am sitting by myself, trying to make sense of the mad world into which I was born. Expunging my mother from the photo was a conceit on my part. It made me look so prematurely wise, I thought. But either way, the photograph cuts straight to the heart of my childhood. I grew up in a household where everything was at once commonplace and completely aberrant.

What defined my childhood years was the choice my parents had made about how they would lead their lives. My father and mother both had master's degrees, his in psychology, hers in social work. That might have positioned us as solidly middle-class. But my father, the son of a Montreal rabbi, was not practising his profession. Instead, he was a full-time organizer for the Communist

Party of Canada, known after the Second World War as the Labour-Progressive Party. He devoted his waking hours to the cause of social revolution. My mother, the daughter of a Protestant clergyman, was a member of the Party in her own right. In tune with the times, she stayed home to keep house and raise the kids. But her spare time was devoted to the work of the Party.

It was not unusual in the 1940s and 1950s for the father to be the head of the household in a way that would seem antique today. My father was much more than that. He was our leader, our guide in an alien world. He provided us with our moral compass. My relationship with him was the axis around which all else in my childhood revolved.

As a child, I loved my parents without reservation. We were part of a tiny, vulnerable group, and they were my guardians against the dangers that threatened to close in on us at any moment. Those threats drove us closer together as a family. They also gave me the idea that we were more important than other families, more truly knowing. It was as though we were early Christians surrounded on all sides by pagans.

One

A SCHOOL DAY

I AWOKE TO THE SOUND of my father calling out to me with a strange little ditty. "School, school, time to go to school," he sang. In his tenor, he made it sound like "Squil, squil, time to go to squil." He was being playful, but the words filled me with trepidation. I was well aware as I saw his head silhouetted in the doorway that this was the day I'd be going to kindergarten for the first time.

Downstairs a few minutes later, I sat across from my father at the little table in the kitchen. My mom was standing by the stove. Usually there were four of us at the table for meals, but my brother Gord, lucky him, was still asleep in the bed next to mine. He was two years old. Now that I was nearly five, I had to go to school.

My father was looking through the morning paper, twisting the corner of his moustache between his index finger and his thumb. He glanced up at me once or twice while he ate his porridge, but he was off on his own mental journey — lost in thought about important things, I imagined. After a couple of minutes, he was back on his feet, picking up his thin brown leather briefcase and leaning down to kiss my mother on the lips. "Goodbye, Quennie," he said, employing his favourite term of endearment for her. Quentin was her maiden name. Pausing as though he had just thought of my presence again, he flashed a smile at me. "You'll enjoy school, Jimmy," he said reassuringly. And then he was out the door, without a coat on this warm morning.

Left alone with my mom, I felt even more insecure, tempted to call on her sympathy and beg off going to school. I wouldn't have dared throwing myself on my father's mercies, but my mother was soft-hearted, and she didn't mind acknowledging the weaknesses of others. My panic lifted, however, and in silence we left the house on Flora Street and walked the three blocks to the neighbourhood public school. Gord toddled along with us, having been roused by my mother at the last moment. It was September 1946.

Our family had moved to Ottawa from Toronto the previous year. My father, a first lieutenant in the Canadian army, had been honourably discharged after two years in Britain and a few post-war months in Germany. Out of the army, my father returned to full-time work for the Communist Party of Canada, whose name had been changed to the Labour-Progressive Party in 1943.

Flora Street was a great place to lose yourself in a kid's world, which is what I did much of the time. I enjoyed riding my tricycle, steering my wagon along the sidewalk with a knee on board and the other leg providing the power, climbing the neighbours' fences, and playing ball, tag and hide-and-go-seek with the kids on the block. But I also lived in the shadow world of my parents' politics. Or maybe it was the other way around. Maybe my real world was the one my parents inhabited, and Flora Street the shadow world where I tried to fake it as a normal kid.

The idea I got hold of first in this life was that you had to be a different person in each of these worlds. My truest early talent was my unerring knack for sliding from role to role, playing each one with complete sincerity. Whatever happened, I knew I must try not to let my worlds collide, though often they did just that.

In a North American Communist family during the Cold War,

truth was a slippery commodity. Communists, my father and my mother included, were masters at disguising the truth. They were not sociopaths; far from it. They were true believers in a faith that was widely reviled. And their faith held that the morality of everyday society was a fraud, one put in place to keep people from challenging the powers that be. To stretch the truth, to lie if necessary, to have a secret life from which you carefully excluded almost everyone—all of this was fine provided it served the higher truth, the higher purpose to which your waking hours were dedicated.

Lying about the things kids normally lied about, however, was frowned on in my family. My parents expected me to tell the truth about whether or not I had punched my little brother or abandoned him. My mother told me sternly almost every day that I was to play with Gord. Not wanting to be stuck with him, I invented a game called "Run on Gord," in which the other kids and I would run away and leave my brother by himself on the street. If I denied playing the game after Gord came home in tears to complain, she got very cross. "I don't like a little liar," she would say.

Every day, I looked forward to the moment when my father would come striding in for dinner, dressed in his suit and tie and carrying his briefcase. He was skinny and energetic, with a large round head, an expansive face and pale skin. His big cornflower-blue eyes were strong enough to contend with a nose that was larger than it was imperious. He had a mellifluous voice that made him sound important. It was a voice that ruled, that made us feel confident he was the man to get us through, whatever happened. My father cast a spell over the people around him. His natural authority and his conviction that he was always in the right made others defer to his opinions, which he was never shy about sharing.

In the kitchen was my pretty mom, with her red lipstick and her brown hair falling to just above her shoulders. While she cooked, she warned Gord and me to be quiet when our father came home.

"He's had a busy day," she would repeat, in her daily mantra. "He's very tired, and he has to go to a meeting later tonight." She was a worrier, always concerning herself with what seemed like small things, dust in the living room that she thought was making her sick, what her sister Margaret had said to her on the phone. For her, reality began with how things affected her, not with how things were. My father never made light of her anxieties. Instead, he played the part of the calmly assured husband.

As they walked down the street arm in arm, alongside my brother and me, my father and mother appeared bright and attractive, a couple anyone would like to know. Nobody looking at them would assume there was anything out of the ordinary. But beneath that deceptive ordinariness was a web of secrecy that affected our every moment. During much of the Second World War, the Communist Party had been illegal in Canada. Leading Communists like my father were on the run from the police.

I felt a little queasy that morning when my mother, Gord and I arrived at our destination. The school was a red-brick three-storey affair with a grassy field off to one end. At the side of the building was a chute that connected the third floor of the school to the pavement. I assumed nervously that if there was a fire, we would all have to slide down the chute to safety.

It was a topsy-turvy scene, with grave little children and crying mothers kissing them goodbye. As we approached the stairs to the big front doors, my mother held my hand. She reminded me about the problem with my birthday. For the past couple of days I had known we were going to lie about my birthday when we got to the school. My mother had coached me carefully to go along with it.

I had not been entirely luckless in the timing of my birth. I entered the world at 5:00 am on December 22, 1941, one day after the birthday of the General Secretary of the Communist Party of the Soviet Union. Six hours earlier and I would have come in on

Joseph Stalin's sixty-second birthday, which would certainly have prompted my proud parents to name me after the great leader.

To be enrolled in kindergarten, though, I had to be five years old by September 1. My parents' solution was to fake my birthday. Somehow my mother managed to convince the school that I had actually been born on August 22. She never told me why it was so important that we lie about the date of my birth, though I figured at the time that it had something to do with my father's work and my mother's own political activities. After this day, from the ages of five to fifteen, I would tell my neighbourhood friends that my birthday was August 22 and have a birthday party each year on that date. I celebrated my real birthday on December 22 with my family.

In the school office, my mother stood at the counter and spoke to a stern-looking older woman who wore thick glasses. The lie about my birthday went off without a hitch. But my trials were not over yet. A younger, fair-haired woman came out from behind the counter and led me by the hand to a table that stood very low off the floor. She sat me down in a little chair and showed me five or six thick pieces of paper, coloured red, blue and green, that were cut out in the shape of flower petals. She handed me a black piece of paper with a circle pasted on it and asked me to arrange the petals around the circle to make a flower in bloom. I tried, but I couldn't get the petals to fit properly. Years later, my mother told me that I had nearly been denied admission to the school for failing this elementary aptitude test.

I would soon learn that school consisted mostly of sitting quietly while the teacher taught us songs or showed us how to draw pictures. I couldn't see the point of any of this, and I couldn't wait until it was time to go home. One day our teacher had us play a game in which each pupil was paired with a partner. My partner was Susan, a girl with large brown eyes. Susan had to sit on the floor while I sat on a chair. Her job was to fold a piece of soft cardboard several times and then hand it to me so that I could fold it a few more times. Whichever team succeeded in making a hat first won the game. Susan and I didn't get far. While she fumbled with the cardboard, I talked to her about playing together after school. I could invite her to my birthday party, I thought, and then remembered that I wouldn't be having a party with my friends until the following August.

IN ONE OF MY STRONGEST early memories, I am hiding behind the satiny, floor-length drapes in the big living room in my maternal grandparents' house in North Toronto. With mounting dread, I am waiting for my father to be welcomed into the house. It is the late autumn of 1945. He has just returned from two years overseas in the Canadian army, and I have not seen him yet. I know from my mother that he came home from England in uniform on a troop ship that landed at Halifax. Gord and I have spent the past week with my grandparents so my parents can get reacquainted on a second honeymoon. Gord, not yet two, will be meeting our father for the first time. He dances gaily on the carpet and does not seem to realize that this is the time for an Oedipus complex to emerge.

I know I am supposed to be full of joy that my father is back. While he was away I often sat and looked at his picture, putting it down beside my toys while I played. I even dragged his slippers around the house with me. But now I am filled with shyness and foreboding. My brother and I are used to having our mother all to ourselves. Yet when the strange man in the uniform walks into the living room with my mother and scoops me up in his arms, I am relieved.

But the joy I was supposed to feel never came. Or at least, it was far from unalloyed. Now that my father was back, I was beginning to learn about him for myself, rather than through my mother's stories. When I sat with him, I often felt his warmth. He captivated me like no other person could. He made me feel safe; as long as we followed him, I knew all would be well. He told me stories about his days in the army and his childhood growing up in Montreal, and he spoke with hope about the better world that was coming. But in a flash, and with almost no warning, his warmth could vanish. He would tense, his face would redden, and then he would lash out at me, my brother or something he had just read in the paper. He had a short-fuse temper that exploded whenever he felt he had been crossed. At first, I couldn't anticipate what would set him off. It could be my tardy arrival at the table for dinner, or some nasty thing I'd said to Gord. His anger reduced his usually rich voice, and his normally kind tone, to a rasping whisper. When I was his target, my pulse quickened and I felt unsteady in the head. When he blew his top, he usually spanked us.

My father's outbursts were spectacular, but not frequent. My mother's temper was less brutal, but she was often angry at my brother and me. She spent more time with us, and that made her more inclined to spank us. Sometimes my parents spanked us with an open hand, sometimes with the back of a hairbrush, a favoured (and painful) instrument for corporal punishment in many families. I didn't give the spankings much thought. They were a part of daily life for not only us but all our friends on the street.

One day shortly after his return, I was in the kitchen with my mother when my father came in and sat down. I can't remember why, but he was furious with me. He glared at me from across the table, the intensity of his anger rising visibly. The tense silence was broken when he shouted that he was not sure we would be able to live together. Was I going to be left on my own? I wondered for a terrified moment. I had been warned by my mother that I was on trial with my father, that I would have to earn his affection. It was not something I could simply count on.

As the years passed, I became more accustomed to my father's evil temper. I even found it amusing, especially if it was directed at someone else. Gord was frequently the target. When I saw that

Like other small children on our street, my brother and I were expected to do chores and run errands for our family. At the age of four, I was sent to the corner, with a couple of empty milk bottles, to buy fresh quarts of milk. Gord was sent when he was only two. I remember him in a blue snowsuit, the snow on either side dwarfing him, trooping back to the house with a quart of milk covering the whole front of his little body, his cheeks red in the cold.

In winter, my brother and I often jumped out the back bedroom window on the second floor into giant mounds of snow. In the living room downstairs, there would be a Christmas tree at the appropriate time. Communism did not stop my parents from celebrating Christmas, a tradition that obviously did not come from my father's side of the family. Christmas in our house centred on Santa Claus. For many years, my father dressed the part in a red dressing gown stuffed with pillows, sporting a white cotton-batten beard attached with Scotch Tape. We would sit in the living room by the tree, impatient for his arrival. To heighten our anticipation, he would clang spoons together to make the sound of an approaching sleigh. At last, he would enter the room with a loud "Ho, ho, ho," which drew shrieks from us for him to distribute the presents.

Our pagan Christmas was completely conventional, with one exception. Gord, Linda and I were told from our earliest days that Santa Claus was a make-believe character. It was one thing for Communists to play at Christmas, but they were vigilant about ensuring that their children did not believe in fairy tales. That included exposing other bourgeois pretenders such as the Tooth Fairy and the Easter Bunny.

Christmas on Flora Street was also the occasion for stories of a disturbing sort.

My father's main job in Ottawa was to find housing for veterans who had been demobilized and were making their way back into civilian life. There was a severe housing shortage across the country, including in the nation's capital. Working through an organization called the Veterans' Housing Association, my father and the organization's firebrand leader accomplished this task in the most spectacular ways, with a keen eye for the excitement and controversy they could generate in the press.

The Veterans' Housing Association would put out the word, through flyers and via the grapevine, that veterans needing homes should assemble with their families and their belongings at a particular time and place. At the appointed hour, my father and the other organizers appeared with trucks. They loaded the vehicles with men, women and children, including infants, and ragtag collections of possessions. Then this unlikely caravan would set out through the streets of Ottawa, followed by police cars. The trucks snaked around the city, playing a cat-and-mouse game with the police, keeping their destination top secret. Finally, they would speed toward their target, usually a government building or a military facility. When they reached their destination, they began moving the homeless people inside as quickly as possible, mothers and babies first. By the time the police arrived to try to stop the occupation, it was too late. Once people were bedded down in their makeshift quarters, on occasion right in the midst of top-secret military equipment, the police did not dare to touch them. The public, firmly on the side of the homeless veterans, was not put off by the association's tactics. In some cases, families stayed in these commandeered quarters for up to two years.

By our Christmas tree in the living room, I heard stories of these struggles to find housing. One night my parents' friend Ruth, a tall woman with bowed shoulders, long stringy hair and the hint of a lisp, gave us a grisly account of a mother and father and their three children burning to death in a flimsy cabin in the Ottawa Valley. A faulty wood stove, the sole source of heat in the cabin, was the culprit. The family's Christmas tree had caught fire, and their little dwelling exploded in flames before any of them could escape. Later, I replayed in my mind images of trapped people choking on smoke.

That same Christmas season we heard about a demonstration held on Parliament Hill in support of the Veterans' Housing Association. (A few weeks earlier my parents had taken me to another demonstration on the Hill. I believe it was my first. Someday I'd like to see my life in pictures, as captured by the Mounties at the demonstrations I've attended over the decades.) Demonstrators had thronged across the lawn in front of the Centre Block and up onto the pavement. As they did so, police charged them on foot. On the pavement, RCMP officers in squad cars drove into the crowd. One police car had headed straight for my mother, and as she moved out of the way, the car turned to pursue her. She changed direction, but the car followed and kept coming at her. The police had tried to run my mother down. I was in shock as I listened.

The story about the police car and my mother made me hate the police. Deep in my bones, I feared the sight of a uniform. Those who wore them were the enemy. One summer night I went for a walk with Gord and a child who lived next door. The three of us made our way onto busy Bank Street. We crossed the street, played on the sidewalk and ran past the storefronts. Suddenly, we were lost.

A black police car came alongside us and stopped. It was a high, old-fashioned vehicle with a running board. The officer climbed out and walked slowly toward us. He looked immensely tall. "You kids seem lost," he said. "Do you need a ride home?" I had no idea how to get home, but I didn't want the policeman to know where we lived. I turned to Gord and whispered an idea to him. Then, pointing at our friend, I said to the policeman, "If you take us to his place, we can find our way home from there." We climbed into the back seat of the car and the policeman drove us to our friend's place. Of course, our friend's house was right next door to ours. But I felt good about pulling a fast one on the cops.

Two

MELITA STREET

IN THE SUMMER OF 1947, the Party decided to move my father to Toronto. One afternoon the moving van came, and soon our house on Flora Street was bare and looked rather sad.

My mother tucked Gord and me into the upper berth of a sleeping car on the dark night we left Ottawa. The shuffling motion of the train and the rhythmic click of the wheels soothed me to sleep. It was sunny when we emerged from Union Station in the early morning. From the station's lower level, I looked up in wonder at the cars driving on the street above. Across the way, the massive grey front of the Royal York Hotel swept up toward the sky.

We moved into a three-storey semi-detached house at 226 Melita Street, in the heart of the city. For some reason, everybody called it Melita Street, although the name on the street signs was Melita Avenue. I liked the look of this red-brick house the first time I saw it. It felt solid, and it had many more rooms than our house on Flora Street. Using the money from a veteran's loan for my father, my parents managed to make a down payment on the house, which they bought for $8,800. And there was more than enough room for us to take in tenants on the first and third floors.

Melita Street would become my true boyhood home. I soon knew every inch of the dead-end street where we lived, each garbage can and alleyway and all the hiding places along the lanes behind the houses. I knew how to find the hollyhocks where you could ensnare bees in bottles fitted out with breathing holes in the lids. I knew where the best rocks were for throwing. To my eyes it was a perfect firmament, and it contained all the things I could possibly need for a life of distractions and adventures.

In our new neighbourhood, factory whistles sounded on all sides at noon, some of them deep and low, others high and piercing. Trains rattled along the CPR line next to Dupont Street, shaking our house more than a block away. Horses clopped down Melita pulling carts of various kinds. In addition to the delivery men who brought bread, milk and ice for people's ice boxes, there was a junk dealer with a long wispy beard calling out for junk in a shrill, melancholic voice as he urged his ancient horse with its drooping head along the pavement. We liked to feed the horses lumps of sugar, taking care not to come in contact with their dripping mouths and their large brown teeth.

Melita Street was teeming with kids, most of whom were being raised in the classic two-parent families of the fifties. The mothers usually stayed home while the fathers went off to work early in the morning. Many of the men carried lunch pails, although some worked in plants or stores close enough for them to walk home for lunch. They were printers, carpenters, factory workers, truck drivers and owners of small shops. Some women on the street also had jobs, and I'd see them coming home in the late afternoons with kerchiefs tied around their heads.

There were no fast-food joints in those days, and people rarely went to restaurants, but sometimes my mom visited the little lunch counter at the corner of Dupont and Bathurst, a few blocks away, to savour a cup of coffee. On Saturday mornings, she would often take

us up to the public library, about a mile away, and we would stop
in at Woolworth's for chocolate milkshakes. We loved to sit on the
stools next to the counter.

Everybody bought their food and other household goods at the
corner grocery store and the local pharmacy. Our corner store,
up at Christie and Davenport, was called Johnson's. You could
buy vegetables and bread and cans of just about everything there.
Mr. Johnson, bald head perspiring, dark-brown stains on his work
apron, spent most of the day in the back of the store, sawing pieces
of meat. The stores also delivered, hiring any kid with a bicycle who
wanted to make a little money.

On weekends, Melita Street was a beehive, humming with
activity. The men, oily rags in hand, devoted hours to lying under
and stooping over their vehicles, an amazing collection of mostly
second-hand cars. Women spent a lot of time with their hair up
in curlers, talking over the back fence to their neighbours or chatting from one porch to the next, often with babies in their arms.
Mrs. B., our next-door neighbour, was a large cheerful woman who
loved to talk. Whenever my mother made the mistake of going out
on our front porch, Mrs. B., whose husband worked at a local factory, would pin her down with long monologues about daily life.
A favourite tactic of hers was to utter the phrase "As I always say,"
then pause just long enough to draw a deep breath before continuing, never allowing her listener to get in a word. My mother finally
learned that the only way out was to claim she could hear her phone
ringing and dash off.

On Melita Street, most of the adults smoked. My mom smoked
when she was with her friends, but never by herself. My father was
the odd man out; he'd smoked one cigarette at age thirteen, and it
made him feel dizzy and sick. He never smoked again. But a friend's
plump father told us one day, when he came home from his job
driving a streetcar, that he was going to take up smoking so he

could lose some weight. We'd been taught in school that England's King James I was a flawed monarch, not least because he believed that smoking tobacco was a filthy habit and bad for the lungs. Poor, delusional King James, we thought. We laughed at him. Where did he get such a strange idea? Butter, cheese, eggs and red meat were regarded as highly healthful foods. Bacon grease sopped up with a piece of bread was prized as a delicacy.

The autumn we moved to Melita Street, I was enrolled in grade one at McMurrich Public School. The school was up on a hill, about three-quarters of a mile from our house. I walked to school with the other kids on the street.

One afternoon, I was sitting at the desk in my classroom, nibbed pen in hand. Ink stains were spattered on my fingers. I dipped the pen in the inkwell and scratched it across the sheet of paper in front of me. It sputtered. I scraped the nib on my blotter, then, in frustration, raised my pen in the air.

Standing right above me, peering down with her intense little eyes, was Miss Pethick. She ordered me to hand her the pen. I passed it to her nib first, which deeply offended her. She gasped and clasped the pince-nez hanging over her large bosom, holding them up to gaze through at me. Her wrists were thick and starchy white. "Sir!" she exclaimed, and ordered me out into the hall. She left me standing there while she went next door and called Miss Winterborne out of her class. Miss Winterborne bent over me to deliver a stern lecture on the horrors of handing a pen to someone nib first. I have never made the mistake since. Miss Pethick, formidable though she was, could not administer a tongue-lashing in the manner of her larger colleague.

Miss Winterborne and Miss Pethick drove to school together each morning. Miss Winterborne was tall and stout, whereas Miss Pethick was short and stout. We did imitations of them getting out of the car; when Miss Pethick stepped out her side went up appreciably, but when Miss Winterborne got out, her side positively surged upward.

Miss Winterborne led the school choir, the pride of McMurrich. Every pupil served in the choir for a time. For weeks we would rehearse our songs for the night the parents came to hear us. Miss Winterborne would hurl her large body about with enormous energy during the songs. Her favourites were emotional outpourings by Stephen Foster about the Old South. Our version of "Old Black Joe" was heart-rending.

Most of the teachers at McMurrich were women who appeared extremely aged to me. I assumed that many of them had lived in the time of Queen Victoria, if not actually known her personally. They wore long skirts and blouses that covered every inch of their anatomy except their fingers and heads, although occasionally you would glimpse a whole hand or a flash of throat. As we sat at our desks writing, teachers would inspect our penmanship. When one teacher told me I had the worst penmanship in the class, I placed my exercise paper on my head with my ink-stained hands. "You might as well leave it there," the teacher remarked. I looked around at the girls in the class, who sat contentedly with their hands folded. How did they manage to print so neatly? I wondered.

The Misses Pethick and Winterborne were Anglo-Canadians, solidly British in their demeanour. In Miss Pethick's class we were taught to draw the Union Jack to perfection, in all its glorious red, white and blue. The Red Ensign with the Canadian coat of arms in the fly and the Union Jack in its corner, flew from our school's flagstaff. When Miss Pethick talked about the United States she referred to the country with a touch of a sneer as the "Thirteen Colonies." At McMurrich, we knew we were Canadians, but we knew we were British as well.

The school was the fulcrum of my neighbourhood, but no one there ever tried to figure out what made us tick. The school didn't care if you had emotional problems. It didn't take an interest in your attitude toward other children or in the attitudes of other children toward you. If you misbehaved in a flagrant way, you would be strapped. Strappings were solemn occasions. We sat gravely still in our seats as the teacher, holding a black thing that looked like a slab of licorice, led the miscreant, always a boy, into the cloakroom. Then we waited for the thwack, followed by another and another, wondering if the boy would cry, as he sometimes did.

My father was paid fifty dollars a week for his work as a Communist organizer. That meant we were far from rich, or even middle-class. Our family didn't own a car, although my father sometimes borrowed cars from his friends. In one sense, we were similar to the other families on Melita Street. Like most of them, ours was a one-income family, with our father going out to work and our mother working at home, raising children. Both my parents had post-graduate university degrees, though, while only a few of the neighbours had any education past high school. What made us really different, of course, was that my father's full-time occupation, the central passion of his life, was to transform the social order.

That my father was a Communist organizer did not strike me as peculiar. I was born in the midst of my parents' political struggles, and I accepted them as the way things were. But I realized early on that Melita Street provided me with another space. I did what I could to keep these worlds separate from one another. I never thought about whether it was right or wrong to mislead people in one world about what went on in another. It was a sheer question of survival. Above all, I was determined to protect the space in which I lived from being contaminated by the politics of my parents.

In many ways, my father was not what I imagined a father was supposed to be. I rarely told him about my troubles, about my aches and pains or who had beat me up in the schoolyard that day. He was not the kind of dad who would go out and play street hockey with you; he might have thrown a ball to me two or three times over the course of my childhood. But although politics drove my father's life, he was not without his lighter side. His indulgences included a vast, if intermittent, appetite for ice cream and chocolate cake. He was fond of lounging on our chesterfield, with pillows propping up his head. Even the onset of back problems, which drove him to see a chiropractor for years, did not wean him from this habit. Above all, my father loved to laugh. If one of us told him a story that was even moderately amusing, casting some person or event in an absurd light, he would laugh until tears came to his eyes and his sides grew sore. He hated board games and card-playing, but he did have a fondness for chess, although he rarely played. He was intrigued by the game's intricacies because he was so good at math — he could multiply and divide long rows of numbers in his head. But he also undoubtedly thought well of chess because it was a favourite Bolshevik pastime, much prized by Lenin among others. My father didn't like chit-chat or gossip, regarding small personal exchanges with disdain. And he was affectionate to a point; he would always give my mother a showy kiss on the lips when he got home, and he would hug me and my siblings as well. But he liked his physical distance.

My mother was my real source of comfort. I could confide in her about my worries, and she would enfold me in her arms and make me feel safe. She knew how to switch things from the large, difficult world of my father to a smaller realm where what counted was intimate and immediate. She would take me out with her to our tiny backyard, where she was trying to coax life into a rosebush climbing a trellis in the shadow of the garage. She taught me songs that she had learned at camp as a girl, songs about paddling a canoe and tenting under the stars.

My mom would cook dinner or wash clothes and put them through the hand wringer as I sat nearby reading comics I'd bought

We were always to be mindful of the burdens that women bore, he instructed my brother and me. This message was not intended as a mere abstraction. It was a directive. We were to be thankful that we had such a wonderful and loving mother, and under no circumstances were we to be critical of her. The theme of how lucky we were to live in this household was drummed home as though it were the central truth of a great cause.

My mother suffered from recurring fears about her health, shifting her focus from one possible ailment to another. For a time, she was highly sensitive about a skin condition that she thought made her cheeks turn red. One evening the family was having dinner in the room behind the kitchen, which served sometimes as a bedroom, sometimes as a dining room. The setting sun suffused the sky with pink. For some reason, my mother had served a couple of glasses of a light pinkish wine with dinner. It must have been some kind of special occasion for my parents.

I gazed across the table at my mother. Feeling rather gallant, I told her she looked very healthy, adding, "Your cheeks are glowing." Her face froze. For a long moment, she stared at me. Then she pushed back her chair, and I could see her choking with tears. She ran from the room, leaving me with my father and brother.

My father tore into me. "How could you do such a thing to your mother?" he thundered. He rushed out of the room as I sat in lonely terror. Our family dinner, with its little pretensions, was over. Later, I had to apologize for what I had done.

Afterward, when my father talked to me about the incident, he drove home his message once more. What you did was terrible, he said, because you are lucky to have such a wonderful mother. Don't ever do it again. His was a very traditional view of women, repackaged to seem revolutionary and up-to-date. Implicit in his message was the idea that women were always worrying about small things, making sure that the house was clean and the groceries had been bought. It was up to men to operate on a loftier plane, concerning themselves with the future of the human race.

I held a special place in this household where so much emphasis was put on changing the world. It was obvious that my father had selected me as his chief disciple. By the time I was five or six, he was explaining the theory and practice of revolutionary politics to me. I knew that he meant these conversations seriously and that their goal was to enlist me in his struggle. It swelled my head to feel I had such an important role to play. But could I live up to his expectations? I wondered anxiously. And would his feelings for me diminish if I could not?

One cold day, my father took my brother and me to the outdoor skating rink in the park above the corner of Christie and Davenport. As he hurried away, I sat down in the snow and pulled on my skates. Then I helped Gord to tie on his two-bladed skates, his learners. I skated around the rink while keeping an eye on my brother, who would walk on his skates, sit down and then haul himself to his feet to try again. We stayed on the ice as the short afternoon turned to dusk.

At last my father reappeared, and we took off our skates and walked home with him. Our mother was in the hospital, he informed us, where she was about to have a baby. Gord and I had been well aware of this impending event. That night, we slept at our grandparents' house. The following morning, over breakfast, Gord and I agreed that we wanted a brother and that his name ought to be Steve. I was eating a piece of toast with marmalade on it when Aunt Margaret came into the dining room to tell us we had a baby sister.

Three

THE SECOND SECRET

AS TEACHERS WENT, I WAS quite fond of Mrs. Anderson, who taught my grade two class at McMurrich. She wasn't bombastic or formal, and she seemed to care about the pupils under her direction. She read stories to us, beginning in the morning and continuing after lunch. Some of them were so exciting I could hardly wait for lunch to end. One I particularly liked involved a boy and a magic machine that made doughnuts.

One morning Mrs. Anderson announced to our class, "We are going to do something very special today. We're going to find out more about each other." That didn't snap me out of the semi-doze I often affected in the classroom. But the next thing she said might as well have been an electric shock: "I am going to ask each of you to tell the class what your father does for a living." By the time I had recovered enough to focus, the third pupil in the first row was on his feet saying that his father was a printer. He sat down, and the girl behind him was getting up. I didn't have long to figure out what to do.

I knew perfectly well what my father did for a living. He was paid by the Communist Party to train other comrades, promote the Party line in the trade unions, agitate for nuclear disarmament and run as a candidate for public office. He was on the Central

Committee, which was not the inner sanctum of the Party leadership, but close to it.

What was I going to do when Mrs. Anderson got to me? What could I tell the class? I knew I couldn't tell the truth, but I didn't know what else to say. My parents had never instructed me explicitly not to reveal what my father did for a living; they didn't have to. I had received the message in a thousand different ways, particularly from my mother, that the Party was engaged in very important work that was highly unpopular with many people. The less said about it, the better. As the teacher worked her way methodically up and down each row, we heard about plumbers, truck drivers, carpenters and fathers who ran butcher shops. I hoped against hope that recess would come, or a fire alarm.

Finally, she got to me. "What does your father do, Jimmy?" Mrs. Anderson asked.

Everyone turned to look at me as I stood silently on my feet.

"I don't know," I stammered.

"You don't know? You must know. What does your father do?" She sounded as though she believed I was being deliberately difficult.

I was in misery. For a long time, I stood by my desk. "He works in an office at 274 College Street," I said at last, "and I can tell you his phone number." I actually blurted out the number.

I rushed home after school to tell my mother what had happened. She stiffened and looked cross. She said it was a political outrage. What right did the school have to query pupils about the occupations of their fathers? What if there was a poor child in the class whose father was unemployed? Wouldn't he or she feel humiliated in front of the others?

Frankly, I didn't give a shit about that. I was the one who was trapped between my parents and my teacher. Strangely, as it turned out, my brother had had a virtually identical experience that day in his kindergarten class. He, too, had not known what to say.

The next morning my mother handed each of us a letter to give to our teachers. In it, she protested what had happened the day before. She concluded by saying that my father was a freelance journalist. Ironically, now that I was prepared to answer it, I was never asked the question again.

Luckily for me, my mother's letter didn't turn Mrs. Anderson against me. She decided I was doing well enough that I should accelerate by completing three grades over the next two years.

DURING THE YEARS OF THE KOREAN WAR, which broke out in June 1950, my brother and I made our pocket money by delivering the *Toronto Star* six days a week and the *Star Weekly* on Saturdays. With the money we earned we bought our bicycles (in instalment payments for a full year), comics, candy and soda pop. We netted about two dollars each a week after we'd collected from our customers and paid the newspaper. Most of our customers were friendly people who even tipped us from time to time. But there were a few who did not mind haggling over twenty-five cents here and there. One customer who thought I delivered his paper late used to tell me he wanted it "when it was news, not history." He liked that line and puffed himself up as he repeated it. When customers failed to pay us, the money came out of our earnings.

My brother and I, as we joked at the time, were the only kids on our street to cheer for North Korea during the war. Every afternoon, as we opened our bundle of papers with a wire cutter, we could check how many North Korean MiGs had been shot down and how many U.S. Sabre Jets had been blown out of the sky. We kept a tally: three hits for our side, four for theirs.

Newspapers and comic books of the day portrayed the North Koreans and the Chinese as a subhuman yellow peril. It was the same in the movies, which continued the tradition of Hollywood films about the war against Japan. Tall white Americans fought a sly and treacherous enemy, on territory populated by hordes, not by people.

At no time was the Red Menace feared more than during the Korean War. The threat was portrayed as having an external side, but there was a great deal of talk about Communist subversion at home. The 1951 film *I Was a Communist for the FBI* portrayed a man who infiltrated the ranks of U.S. Communists to tip off the authorities about planned acts of sabotage. Later came the weekly television drama *I Led Three Lives,* which had a similar plot line. In these dramas, Communists were depicted as spies. The red double agent, who was really working for the FBI, was always meeting with Commie higher-ups who were planning to dynamite some vitally strategic industrial facility.

I liked these shows, and I identified with their version of good guys against bad guys, just as I did when I read Korean War comic books. The fact that this contravened my family's most cherished beliefs didn't bother me. It was as if the shows and the comics were in a separate compartment, entertainment. In a society where almost everybody hated what my parents believed in, I was in no position to be choosy about the messages conveyed on television or at the movies. The term "Cold War" was already in use, but the phrase on everyone's lips was "Iron Curtain." Europe was divided between a Western and a Soviet sphere, and a desperate battle was underway between those on opposite sides. To make matters worse, according to the popular wisdom, Stalin's side made use of Communist Party members to act as a fifth column in countries like Canada and the United States.

To mobilize their forces in this highly polarized setting, Communists were fond of marching through the streets and holding outdoor rallies. My brother and I and our little sister, Linda, were regular crowd fodder on such occasions. One march and rally, to generate support for public housing, started beside a housing project where emergency dwellings had been put up during the Second World War. Hundreds of us marched along the main streets led by the inevitable sound car, which blared out our message. As we walked on that pale sunlit afternoon, I skirted streetcar tracks and stepped around piles of horse manure.

It was exciting to march and hold balloons. People stood on front porches and sidewalks staring at us as we went by. Most of them looked on blankly, but a few jeered and the odd one waved his fist, shouting that we should all "go back to Russia." When someone jeered I looked away, pasted a smile on my face and tried to behave as though everything was perfect.

The housing procession wound its way to Queen's Park and ended at a bandstand on the grassy circle north of the legislature building. There we were regaled with long speeches by party stalwarts. The speeches were punctuated by the catcalls of university students who had wandered over from the adjacent campus. At one point, a group of students seemed about to charge the bandstand, but Party men surrounded the platform to protect it.

MY FATHER WAS BUSY from early morning to late at night — usually with a break for supper at home — attending meetings, walking picket lines, managing election campaigns and editing newspapers. The party he worked for, still known as the Labour-Progressive Party, was under savage attack from many quarters. In Parliament, Progressive Conservative and Social Credit MPs called for the outright banning of the LPP and of Communist organizations such as the party's National Federation of Labour Youth. In the aftermath of the Gouzenko affair, the federal government had established a sweeping system of security checks. The RCMP investigated tens of thousands of civil servants, scientists, university professors and labour leaders. They were on the lookout for any evidence of political radicalism or of homosexuality; the prevailing theory was that homosexuals in sensitive posts could be blackmailed into handing over government secrets to the enemy.

In defence of his Padlock Act, which gave police the power to seal off any property where they found evidence of Communist literature or activity, Quebec Premier Maurice Duplessis claimed the law protected people "against the vile cocaine of Communism." Speaking at a police veterans' association meeting in Toronto, George Drew, Ontario's Conservative premier, called on Ottawa to ban the LPP, because "a Communist is an agent of a foreign power sowing the seeds of discontent throughout the country." Drew attacked the two LPP members of the Ontario Legislature, J.B. Salsberg and Alex MacLeod, as rats, saying "'Rat' is the only word to use because they are gnawing away at the foundations of our free society."

Even members of the Liberal government, who did not favour banning the LPP, warned of the Communist menace. Prime Minister Mackenzie King proclaimed that there was "no menace in the world that is greater" than Communism. And later, as external affairs minister, Lester Pearson — while expressing the hope that "we may never succumb to the black madness of the witch hunt" — felt moved to say, "Let us by all means remove the traitors from positions of trust." In 1948, sixty-eight per cent of the Canadians polled had declared themselves in favour of outlawing organizations that were "largely Communistic."

Anti-Communism was also virulent in Toronto's local politics. In Ward Five, where my family lived, one of the candidates for the board of education had made anti-Communism the centre of his campaign. Harold Menzies, whose name was often mentioned in our house, was a realtor who had served on the board in earlier years. He distributed a campaign blotter that urged voters to "Keep Communism out of Our Schools." His fight for a seat in 1948 drew wide public interest, because one of the other candidates in the race was Edna Ryerson, a Communist seeking her fourth term on the board. A striking-looking young woman, with dark curly hair piled high on the top of her head, Ryerson was a frequent visitor to our house on Melita Street.

Menzies's campaign flyers claimed that he was the "Only Candidate Not a Communist." It warned voters against apathy: "Your Innocent Children's Future Depends on YOUR VOTE." His crusade did win him a seat on the board, but it did not prevent Ryerson from holding onto hers. In her campaign literature, Ryerson made no reference to the LPP or to Communism. What made her popular with voters was that she championed free milk and hot lunches for the children of poor parents, investments in school safety, and the provision of junior kindergarten. Shortly after his election, Menzies introduced a resolution at a board meeting to deny any "individual, group, or body which is part of, or associated with, the Communist movement" the right to hold meetings in school buildings. While the *Toronto Star* and the *Globe and Mail* opposed the idea that a legally recognized political party could be denied rights afforded to others, the *Toronto Telegram* editorialized in favour of the resolution, arguing that school property should not be "placed at the disposal of those who would destroy Canada as we know it." Despite spirited opposition from Edna Ryerson, Menzies's motion passed by a vote of sixteen to four.

My father ran unsuccessfully several times in the ward next to ours for a seat on the school board alongside Edna Ryerson. I was glad that he was running for school trustee and not some other office, since there was no party label attached to schoolboard candidates on the election flyers or the signs posted up around the ward. This didn't prevent the daily newspapers from identifying him as a Communist candidate, however. I saw the stories in the paper now and then, but in my child's world they were less important than election signs on front porches. I never suspected that anyone on Melita Street, especially the kids, might actually be reading the newspaper stories.

One kid I knew, named Tim, had a father who ran as a Communist candidate in provincial elections. Tim was always being beaten up on his way to school by bullies who called him a Commie. However, as I saw things, Tim was the kind of kid they would have beaten up anyway. Politics was just an excuse. Somewhat introverted, Tim was extremely good at mathematics. And he had perfect pitch; if you played a key for him while he stood behind the piano, Tim could come out and hit the correct key every time. He studied astronomy on his own time, and he taught me the names of the nine planets.

Tim, whose parents were close friends of my parents, had other problems as well. Once my mother came into a room where Tim and my brother were playing to discover that Tim was holding a pillow over Gord's face. Horrified, she tore the pillow off. Tim looked at her oddly. He had been holding the pillow on my brother for only one minute, he said, and it took five minutes to actually smother someone.

While debates raged about the right of Communists to operate as a party, my father's work also plunged him into vicious battles within labour unions. The most savage of these was between pro-Communists and gangsters for control of the union that organized the men who worked on Great Lakes ships. The Canadian Seaman's Union (csu), in which there was a strong Communist presence, was under attack by the American-based Seafarers' International Union (siu). Both the Canadian and the American governments were involved in the campaign to help the siu defeat the Communists. The U.S. Taft-Hartley Act, which barred Communists and other subversives from holding union posts, was used to prevent suspect Canadian unionists from doing their jobs in unions that operated on both sides of the border. Hal Banks, an American with a criminal record, was sent north by the head of the siu to run the Canadian branch of the union. Despite his gangster past, Canadian authorities allowed Banks to enter the country as a landed immigrant. Violence erupted on the ships and the docks as SIU thugs subdued the CSU.

On a Saturday when the temperature broke a hundred degrees, my father drove me down to Welland with him. We went to the local jail to bail out a CSU activist and bring him back to Toronto. The unionist was a sad-looking, thin, balding fellow. I sat in the back seat of the car with him on the way home. He mumbled quietly about being locked up and said he hoped it wouldn't happen to him again. I felt sorry for the little guy.

Based on what I could see of my father's job, though, I concluded that the main way you changed the world was by going to meetings. Full-time Communists like my father seemed to be at them non-stop. Some meetings were with the top leaders of the Party, and these were very significant. Others were with local Party members. And there were meetings with people in the various united fronts, too, non-Communists from the peace movement or the labour movement. Meetings seemed the key to everything.

My view was naïve, but it contained an important element of truth. From the time the Communist Party of Canada was founded at a secret convention in a barn near Guelph, Ontario, in 1921, Canadian Communists went through countless internal debates and struggles. In the beginning, there were actually two parties: a secret party in which the top leaders formulated strategy and a public party that worked in the labour movement and the political arena. The big guns attended both sets of meetings while concealing the existence of the secret party. It must have been confusing. Fortunately, by the time my father came on the scene, there was only one party, although it went through upheavals whenever top comrades returned from Moscow with the latest version of the correct Party line. The line was honed in Moscow's Lenin School, where both pre-eminent and up-and-coming leaders in the world's Communist Parties studied for as long as a year or two. When Canadian graduates returned to Toronto, they often gave the Party's leadership a very hard time, forcing them to recant on matters of incorrect doctrine.

While large meetings were held in halls, smaller meetings were held in houses, and there were many meetings at our home on Melita Street. The Party had hundreds of members in Toronto. Along with Montreal and Winnipeg, the city was a major centre of Communist strength. My parents belonged to one of a number of Party cells in Toronto. On the night of a meeting, Party members began climbing the stairs to our second-floor residence right after supper. I was allowed to visit with them as the living room filled up with people and cigarette smoke. Some members were frequent visitors to our house, and I got to know them well. There was Nick, the carpenter with the wide thick moustache, who seldom said anything. His wife, Margo, was gigantic. I soon discovered that she smelled bad, so I tried not to sit beside her. Margo drove an ancient Ford, and she loved to visit my mother in the afternoons for long gossip sessions about other Party members. Margo was good at stirring up passions, as I saw close up when she addressed a meeting of housewives on the subject of the rising cost of living. She was a street fighter.

My father got involved with one of Margo's crusades when the packaging of milk was switched from glass bottles to disposable paper containers. Both of them suspected a diabolical plot; they were sure that the new containers were dispensing less milk than the old ones had. One Saturday morning, my father stood in our kitchen in his undershirt, pouring water back and forth from a glass milk bottle to a new paper container. He spilled water all over the place, which made his calculations useless. After a couple of hours of this, he was happy to leave the campaign against the milk companies to Margo.

Bill, an ordinary middle-class man, was an aging Party member who sometimes attended meetings with his wife. I once made the mistake of informing Bill that I could tell when people were wearing false teeth, and asked him to open his mouth. When he did so, I was acutely embarrassed to see that he was outfitted with a set of dentures you could spot a mile off. I wondered at times why Bill was a Communist. How was he qualified to belong to a party that claimed its members constituted a tough, resilient, peerless vanguard? The most noteworthy thing he ever did, as far as I knew, was to construct a sailboat in his basement. The difficulty was that he hadn't thought about how he was going to get the boat out. One time when we were over at his house, I went down to take a look. There was the boat, mahogany buffed to perfection. But it was never going near water unless the house could be lifted away from it.

Art was another Party member who came to meetings from time to time. He was tall and thin, with a receding hairline. One Christmas night when we returned to our house from dinner at my grandmother's, Linda, the first through our front door, found Art lying perfectly still in a pool of vomit on the stairs inside. My parents hustled the three of us past him. Convinced, as were my brother and sister, that he was dead, I was much relieved to learn that Art was merely drunk and unconscious. Linda was allowed to sleep on the third floor that night with our tenants, as far away as possible from where our parents' friend was being revived. (Linda suffered in her own special way from the pressures of my parents' involvement in the Party. When she was a tiny child, she played a game in her room with two dolls, preparing her babies to flee from a nameless threat. Even as an adult she has continued to have nightmares about our family escaping from some terrible danger.)

Another Party member was Harry, a high-strung intellectual whose arrival at the house was always awaited with trepidation. Harry was extremely opinionated. He read voluminously and couldn't stop talking. The word was that he suffered from severe problems of "bourgeois individualism." That was a term Communists loved to fling around. All it meant was that someone was opinionated and flighty. On one occasion Harry managed to lock himself out of his car while it was running. With rising hysteria, he fitfully tried each of the doors in vain. Then he abandoned all self-control and ran in circles around the car, crying out for help.

Once a meeting was called to order, my siblings and I had to leave. The buzz of voices curled down the hall to my bed, followed at times by loud exchanges between people and, not infrequently, crescendos of uproarious laughter.

Quite often, in the afternoons, I would sit with my mother and friends like Margo while they dissected these meetings. So-and-so was really out to get me, one of them would say. Inevitably, the conversation would include the words "criticism and self-criticism." I heard that phrase from my mother and her friends as often as I heard about "bourgeois individualism." Indeed, the two phrases were frequently linked. Under the acrid title of "criticism and self-criticism" came the most hotly anticipated feature of the meetings of Communist cells: the moment when the revolutionaries had to don their hair shirts. As shock troops of the revolution, members had to cleanse themselves of deviations and bourgeois tendencies. So, one by one, each member was asked to admit to failings in a frank statement of self-criticism. That was followed by the other members heaping criticisms on the person under discussion, which was followed in turn by the response of the person in the spotlight. The whole thing was modelled rather obviously on the Catholic confessional.

Speeches of self-criticism were stilted affairs in which people confessed to various forms of softness and bourgeois sentimentality. My mother, one of the few WASPs in the cell my parents belonged to, would often come in for drubbing solely for that reason. She would be told that she harboured a snooty attitude toward the others, that she exhibited the vestiges of class prejudice. The day after a meeting, she often complained bitterly about the criticisms she had endured. There was no point in quarrelling with anything said at the meeting — bridling at a criticism was proof positive of how bourgeois you remained. But Margo was particularly thin-skinned about receiving criticism. After one meeting, I heard my mother telling another friend about Margo's response to the hot coals of criticism. "Criticism accepted," Margo had replied stiffly. "Next."

One night, things came to a head with Harry. The air was thick with tense anticipation the evening he was to be drummed out of the Party. His formal crime was "bourgeois individualism," which really meant he was driving his comrades crazy. Other members arrived early and colluded in hushed tones about how to handle the upcoming scene. They seemed to be finding it all quite delicious. (From this vantage point, I'd call it Communist foreplay, leading to the fulfilment of an expulsion.) Finally Harry arrived, and I was whisked off to bed. A short time later I could hear loud speeches. Sometimes it was Harry talking, sometimes the others. Harry's anguished voice pierced the air. He was like a wounded deer, and the pack was on him. We didn't see Harry any more after that.

We also saw our share of prominent Communists at the house on Melita Street. On one occasion, Tim Buck, leader of Canada's Communists, dropped in — a distinct honour. When I came into the living room, he was sitting there in a big armchair. Slight and unprepossessing in appearance, he always wore dull-looking, baggy clothes, a uniform that seemed intended to announce his fitness to lead the working class. He pulled me onto his lap and cuffed me jovially.

In those days, Tim Buck was a household name in Canada. Party members invariably referred to him as "Tim" in a way that suggested intimacy. Buck became famous when he was arrested in 1931 and sentenced to five years in the Kingston Penitentiary. He and seven other Communists were charged under the notorious Section 98 of the Criminal Code, which made the propagation of supposedly seditious ideas a criminal offence. Shots were fired into Buck's cell by prison guards in a failed attempt to kill the Communist leader. A nationwide campaign to set free the jailed Communists bore fruit in the autumn of 1934, when they were released with only half of their terms served. In Toronto, people wanting to see Buck upon his release packed Maple Leaf Gardens, and thousands more had to be turned away.

A flamboyant figure who visited us quite often was Stewart Smith, the LPP member who held a seat on Toronto's board of control, then the highest governing body in municipal politics. During the 1930s, Smith had made his mark in the Party by writing a series of fiery attacks on Canada's social democrats. In one pamphlet, he had called on revolutionaries to "intensify tenfold their exposure of the capitalist theories and program of the CCF." Smith was a rapid talker with a quick mind.

Less well known than Smith was my father's close friend Sam Walsh, a Party organizer who ran regularly as a candidate for the LPP. For a time, he held a seat on Toronto's board of education. Sam was a dark-haired, good-looking man who exuded importance. Whenever he came over, I assumed that meant he and my father would soon be locked away discussing matters of great significance. My father, never fond of pets, used to explain why he never patted Skippy, the family dog, by asking rhetorically, "Do I pat Sam Walsh?"

One thing my brother and I knew well was that a sizable proportion of the population royally hated Communists and the LPP. On occasion, my parents would talk us into delivering Communist flyers or newspapers, like the *Canadian Tribune,* door to door, not far from our house. We made the deliveries at top speed, above all trying to avoid contact with anyone. Sometimes, though, an irate person stormed down the steps and shouted epithets at us as we retreated: "Dirty Commies," or "Don't leave this garbage on my porch." Once, a man confronted me face to face and snarled, "Who gave you this stuff?" I replied that someone had paid me ten cents to deliver the papers.

It was worse when Gord and I were asked to stand on street corners to hand out flyers. Most people took them without comment, but the odd one asked us who the hell we were and where we got this crap. Again, I would fall back on the story that I had been paid to hand the stuff out. On one occasion, when I got tired of taking the heat, I stuffed three-quarters of the flyers in a garbage can and went home. My parents might be on the right side in their politics, I figured, but I was not going to be denounced for their unpopular ideas if I could help it.

During one election campaign, my parents affixed a large Communist sign to the front porch of our house. I did everything possible to keep my friend Bob, who lived a few blocks away, from coming to visit me. Bob's father was an Anglican minister, and I shuddered to think what he would conclude if he saw the Communist sign. I wondered why my parents had bothered to put it up in the first place, since everybody else on our street hated the Party, but I didn't dare say that aloud.

Disaster struck, or so I feared, when Bob came over unannounced to see me. Trying to make the best of a bad situation, I told him that the sign had been put up by the tenants who occupied our first floor. My family would have put up a Conservative sign if we could have, I said. Actually, this was not a total lie; the tenants downstairs were also Communists.

On that same visit, Bob somehow wandered into my parents' bedroom. The room's main feature, unfortunately for me, was a large bookcase filled with the complete works of Lenin and Stalin. There were about twenty volumes with their authors' names starkly emblazoned in gold lettering on the spine. "Those books are about the crimes of Lenin and Stalin," I observed coolly. But I'm not sure Bob had ever heard of either of them.

We weren't always so lucky in avoiding confrontations. Another time, my brother and I were playing cowboys with a friend at his house. As part of the game, we tied Gord up and left him lying on the porch. The door suddenly flew open, and out came my friend's father. When he saw me standing there, he shouted, "That's how they treat people in Russia, but it's not the way we do things here." He went back inside, slamming the door behind him.

Even though my father was away from the house more than most fathers on Melita Street, he sought right from the start to transmit his values to me. Whether we were walking down the street or sitting on a bench in Christie Pits, I liked hearing the stories he had to tell about the world. I felt special when he did this.

He always started by telling me that he was a philosophical materialist. The word "materialist" made me think of rocks, of hard, solid things. In my father's world view, you had to start with the things that were really there, not with mere ideas. He got very excited as he pounded home the message that all correct political thinking was rooted in materialism. Otherwise, you were mired in the shifting sands of philosophical idealism. Even though idealism sounded like a lovely word, I learned from an early age that when a Communist calls you an idealist, it is meant as a crushing insult.

Whether my father talked about Aristotle or Marx, about the Russian Revolution or what Balzac had written about the French capitalists, I found it fascinating. Much of what he said was way over my head, but I always got the drift. However crudely, I wrapped my head around materialism and idealism, the struggles of working people for a better life and the thrilling days of the 1917 Bolshevik seizure of power in Russia. It was candy for the mind.

For my father, the events of everyday life were mundane. While some people might enjoy a sunset or the freshness of a summer evening, his passion was for the ideas he believed held a key to understanding the world. As his oldest child, I was picked as the natural listener for all of this. And I enjoyed it. Taking in what he had to say made me close to him in a way that nothing else did. It was our deepest bond.

Most of my father's lectures to me as a child — and lectures is what they were — were serene and confident in tone. Religion, however, made him deeply angry. My father rejected the existence of God so passionately that it scared me. If there was no God, no harm done, I thought. But if by chance God was there, why risk offending him? As an adult, I concluded that my father's rejection of God had an eighteenth-century air to it, as though he were busy fighting the *ancien régime* in France. Passion about reason may seem contradictory, but my father was a passionate rationalist, a rationalist with a capital R.

Ironically, despite my father's abhorrence of idealism, his conception of progress was rooted in a faith that was as much an idealist projection as any religion. That faith burned strongest when it came to his understanding of human history. He was convinced that Karl Marx had indeed developed a scientific approach to comprehending the historical process. For thousands of years, human history had been the saga of societies in which a dominant social class exploited a dominated class. Capitalism, my father was sure, was to be the last such exploitative system. Capitalism was creating ever more efficient modes of production, but it was also inexorably dividing society into a more and more concentrated capitalist class and a growing wage-earning class. Eventually, the workers would throw off the capitalists, seize control and usher in the first truly human era.

I got a simple version of this view of things from the time I could talk. That version was updated and rendered more complex as I got older, like a growing tree that is taking shape from the time its earliest shoots break the ground. The faith of my father was no more difficult for a child to master than is Christianity or Judaism. In later years, I would hear preachers struggling to explain the Virgin birth or the tragic death of a young person, having a tougher time of it than my father did. The Communist world view was coherent, and it had answers for the great questions of life and existence. I was open to it. I imbibed it, breathed it in and accepted it.

As with all great faiths, Communism's nooks and crannies were discovered only through experience. Problems arose when you began to examine the instrument of the faith — the Communist Party. The Party was essential to the enterprise. As my father explained to me, the working class was not capable of bringing about the revolution on its own. Untutored workers were able to make it as far as what Communists called "trade union consciousness"; they could figure out that the boss was screwing them and that they needed to fight for higher wages and better working conditions. Where they needed leadership of a higher order was in making the step to "socialist consciousness." To become revolutionaries, to rid themselves of crass economic goals, workers had to find their way to the true party of socialism. And the true party of socialism had to prove its indispensable role to the workers.

The Communist Party, my father taught me, was the vanguard of the working class, the instrument of its liberation. Without the vanguard, the job would never get done. My father always talked with reverence about the Party, as though it were a fine, intelligent creation that had managed to rise from the slime of human existence. Even as a ten-year-old, I spotted the great problematic question here: Who decides who is the vanguard? I asked my father that question, and the answer I got was the story of how the torch was passed from one great leader to the next. It turned out, I quickly learned, that the vanguard depended on great leaders. Great prophets, if you like.

First among the living prophets of the new faith was the General Secretary of the Communist Party of the Soviet Union, Joseph Stalin. Much later, when the terrible truth about Stalin and his murderous regime became general knowledge, and was finally accepted even among those who had held the Communist banner high, my father and others tried to refocus the past to make it appear that they had always had doubts about him. But when I was a child, my father conveyed no such doubts to me. Stalin was always presented as a brilliant, shrewd, visionary leader who was without peer in his time. He was, I was told — falsely, I later learned — the chosen successor of Lenin. Lenin was the genius who'd comprehended Marxism not as a doctrine for intellectuals but as a living creed for action, which had made him the man of the hour in the great revolution of 1917. Before Lenin, of course, there had been Engels and Marx.

As far as my father was concerned, Karl Marx was the greatest genius who had ever lived. (Years later I was to hear the caution Marxists always issue, especially to non-believers. Marxism, they claim, is a materialist doctrine that deals with the world as it is, seen without the blinkers worn by those blinded by false consciousness.) Marxists have the ability to understand and interpret the course of history as none before. By definition, therefore, to deify a particular individual — a thinker, a leader — and to discover the world through his thought alone is to stand Marxism on its head. Karl Marx must never be deified, I was taught as a child, but my father also made it clear that no human being had ever approached Marx's matchless insight and intelligence. If this was a mixed message, the underlying sense was clear: Marx was a towering giant. His like had never come before. Communists placed a garland on his head while stoutly denying that anyone should ever wear one.

Other kids had Jesus Christ or Robin Hood to revere, maybe George Washington or Winston Churchill, but few of them lived with those heroes as I did with Marx, Engels, Lenin and Stalin, as though they were omnipresent. Adding to my appreciation of these men was the large number of Soviet novels supplied to me by my parents. A few of the novels were by Maxim Gorky, then prized as the leading Soviet author, but there were many others by lesser lights. The stories often dealt with the terrible civil war that followed the revolution in Russia, the battles between the Reds and the Whites. Many featured scenes in which supporters of the revolution, whom we had come to know in the story, were dragged out to be hanged en masse. There were vivid descriptions of them helping each other up onto the platform, singing together until the end, and then of their bodies left dangling for days afterward.

Other stories dealt with the heroic effort to establish collective farms in the Ukraine despite the wiles of the wealthier farmers, who were known as the kulaks. There were also the adventures of kids in an orphanage run by dedicated Communists, especially of one brave boy named Pavel; the kids endured every kind of hardship and thus were tempered into the steel that goes into making Soviet Communists. For a while, I wanted to be like Pavel. Some books contained tales of Soviet heroes in the fight against the Nazis during the Second World War; one told the story of a pilot who was shot down and had to make his way back to his own lines through the frozen forest. The pilot's feet had to be amputated following his terrible ordeal, but he persevered, retrained and became an ace fighter pilot with many kills to his credit. One novel, about the attempt to introduce Communist ideas to the aboriginal peoples of Soviet Asia, even had a bit of romance in it, but gruesome executions, not steamy couplings, were the main fare.

These novels were intended to shape my mind in a desirable direction. And I got a sharp reminder that my father cared what I thought when I wrote a short adventure story for the kids' page of *Champion,* a Communist newspaper. My completely non-political story featured a dog who got involved in harrowing escapades. For some reason, my dog crossed the border from Canada into the U.S. and ended up in Idaho. My father found this completely unacceptable and made me change it so that the dog found his way to "Southwest Canada," wherever that might be.

Four

THE THIRD LIE

WHEN WE FIRST LIVED THERE, Melita Street was almost entirely Anglo-Canadian Protestant, with a few Catholics thrown in. There was one Jewish family living on Melita, the Silvers. They once invited us over for a visit, and my parents, in an uncharacteristic moment of openness, told their hosts that theirs was a mixed marriage. My father asked the Silvers to guess which of them was Jewish. They promptly guessed that it was my brown-eyed mother.

In the McMurrich School area, about three-quarters of the kids were Christian, the rest Jewish. Almost all of the Jewish kids lived up the hill near the school. I soon figured out that you had to be either Christian or Jewish; nobody wanted you to be both, and neither group accepted half-breeds. Technically, I couldn't be Jewish anyway, because my mother was not. But my father was Jewish, and I carried his name. Laxer is not the most Jewish-sounding name there is, but in Toronto at the end of the forties it stuck out. I looked every inch a Jewish kid, too. I was short and skinny with close-cropped hair (thanks to the local barber, who should have been a butcher), and I had a big nose. It was the kind of nose that the WASP kids associated with Jews. They used to recite a poem about Moses and Jewish kids with long noses.

My mother, a twenty-seven-year-old from an upper-crust WASP Toronto family, had not felt at home in the downtown Montreal Catholic hospital where she delivered me into the world. The Communist Party was illegal at the time, and the Party had dispatched my father to work in Montreal during this perilous period. My parents chose the dingy hospital so that my fugitive father could visit his wife and newborn son without alerting the police. Struck by the shock of black hair that stood straight up on my head, the nurse who carried me in to my mother announced cheerfully, "Your baby looks like a Bolshevik."

The sting of this remark had barely subsided when my poor mother looked up to see my father's sisters arriving to welcome me into the world with a traditional Jewish circumcision. Members of the family had approached several mohels to come down to give me the snip. But the mohels had turned up their noses at the thought of dealing with such non-kosher material. Finally one of the sisters found a nice little man by the name of Dr. Weiner who was prepared to do the deed. At the ceremony, my aunt Elsie was so horrified by my appearance — I think it was the hair — that she had to stuff a scarf in her mouth to stop herself from gasping.

A few months later, this first association with the religion my father had abandoned was countered when I was christened in the chapel of Deer Park United Church in Toronto. When I was old enough to have my own ideas about my unseemly beginnings, I developed the conceit that my real parents were French-Canadian and that it was in error, in the dimly lit halls of the downtown Montreal hospital, that I had been delivered into the care of this odd family. But that thought came to me only after I had witnessed several of the hilariously awkward, and thankfully rare, meetings between my Jewish and my WASP relatives. Together, both sides seemed like pure caricatures, my older Jewish relatives huddled together and speaking with a pronounced intonation from somewhere between Poland and Brooklyn, the WASPs standing impossibly far apart and commenting in their high Ontario dialect on the weather and other weighty matters. In later years, I'd find that my WASP relatives were most alive at funerals, particularly at the receptions following interments, when they summoned up a jaunty cheer that made me feel as if I was attending a Rotary Club luncheon.

In the presence of these two groups, I was caught in the middle. I could blend in perfectly with either the Jews or the WASPs when I was with them on their own. When they got together, though, I was stuck, not knowing which guise to adopt. And I didn't really feel I fit in with either. When I went to Montreal to visit my Jewish relatives, I knew I wasn't Jewish. In Toronto, in the real world where I lived, I couldn't make myself feel exactly like a WASP. I could fake the externals well enough — I spoke perfect WASPy English — but something on the inside of my body was telling me different.

It bugged me that being Jewish meant your nose and your dick looked different. My parents' attitude made matters worse. In our house, it was treated as a deep dark secret that my siblings and I were part Jewish. I don't recall either my mother or my father forbidding us to tell people, but the message was clear: this was something that no one else was to know about. I was getting used to the idea that my life was divided into watertight compartments, however. Some people were to know this but not that, other people were to know more. The world was a tough place, and you had to be very careful what you told anyone.

The decision to raise us as though we were WASP kids fitted in with my father's migration from the Jewish ghetto and his adoption of an anti-religious ideology. Being Jewish was an unnecessary complication, and he wanted no part of it. I think this attitude also helped strengthen my parents' marriage. Since my mother's family lived in Toronto, it seemed simplest for us to be raised as non-Jewish kids who had a vague relationship to the United Church, in which our maternal grandfather was a minister.

The painful days were Jewish holidays. On those occasions, one-quarter of the kids were not present at school. I sat there feeling uncomfortable, sure that everyone was looking at me. Sometimes kids asked me, "Laxer, what the hell are you doing here?" Once Mr. Phalon called me out of the classroom into the hall and said, "Jimmy, why are you at school today? It's a Jewish holiday." "I'm not Jewish," I replied, feeling tight inside, feeling violated and miserable. It was the third big lie of my life.

In hiding my Jewish roots, I was not merely seeking the path of least resistance. Although I scarcely knew it at the time, I was following along my father's path. The way he explained it to me, it was perfectly natural that he should end up a Marxist, committed to the overthrow of capitalist society. The truth was, he had started off as an orthodox adherent of a very different faith.

My father, Mendel Laxer—his first name was actually Menachem, a fact I discovered not long after my fiftieth birthday— was born in Montreal in 1915. His own father and mother, Getzel and Freda, had fled to North America from the eastern reaches of the Austro-Hungarian Empire in 1900.

Getzel, who was a rabbi in the Orthodox Hasidic tradition, was the grandfather I never knew. He died of a heart attack when I was four months old. As a consequence of my unconventional start in the world, my grandfather didn't come to see me, even though he and I were living in the same city at the time. A few months before I was born, word had got out to members of my grandfather's congregation that his son's wife, a non-Jew, was expecting a baby. Six or seven of his followers were so incensed at the news that they gathered outside the family house and pelted my grandfather with tomatoes. My grandfather was deeply ashamed. His daughters had borne many children by this time. But now a son of his, the son he had chosen to be his spiritual heir, was to become a father. Dark stories circulated in the family that the shame of it may have led to his untimely demise.

Whether or not that was true, my grandfather did not join the pilgrimage of family members who came to witness my ritual circumcision. His boycott was not joined by my father's mother, though. Both during my mother's pregnancy and after I was born, my grandmother brought food to my parents' apartment to help out the woman who was having her son's baby. Rumours persist in the family that, just before his death, my grandfather overcame his horror at my birth and decided to have a first meeting with my mother and me. But he died before he could do it.

I suppose I should feel troubled that my grandfather did not choose to see me when he had the chance. In what I have learned of him since, I have found a man much to my liking. The photos my father had of him show my grandfather with an unkempt beard, dressed in black clothes. He looks not unpleasant. But he is terribly distant. How could there be any connection between this strange figure and me? He is beyond my reach, a ghostly figure from the past who set the stage for the outlandish beginning of my life.

My father was the eighth of nine offspring. His brother Max, also known as Jack and sometimes Nick, was seventeen years his senior. After Max came two sisters and another boy. Sadly, the boy died before his first birthday. Then came three more daughters, followed by the arrival of Menachem Mendel. A male baby, after so many females and the boy who had died, made my father's birth a great event in the family. Eastern European Jews doted on blonds, and this blond, blue-eyed newcomer seemed to answer the hopes of his father for a successor. Max had already escaped from his father's grasp. Showing little interest in his studies, my father's older brother had quit school early to run off and join the U.S. army.

My father's mother also extended a warm welcome to the new arrival, so much so that she kept him in her bed until he was about

five years old. Years later my father told me he thought she was calculating that this might reduce the chances of another pregnancy
and yet another mouth to feed. Only with the birth of his sister,
Lily, the last of the line, was Mendel finally evicted from his mother's boudoir.

With doting parents and sisters interpreting his every twitch
and grunt, the blue-eyed baby was reputed to be a genius by the
time he was ten months old, already credited with remarkable
mathematical and linguistic skills. "Did you hear what he just
said?" an ecstatic sister would exclaim when some sound escaped
my father's lips in a room crowded with members of their large
family. By the time he was a small boy, everyone assumed that he
was to be a rabbi.

Mendel attended Hebrew school every day after his classes at
public school had ended. These long hours were wearying and kept
him from playing on the street with other kids. He never learned to
ride a bicycle or to skate. Once, under cover of darkness, I took my
father to the rink at Christie Pits to see if I could teach him to stand
up on skates. By then it was too late. He flailed about helplessly on
the ice, and we dropped the experiment.

Many of my father's teachers were staunch Anglo-Saxon First
World War veterans who had little rapport with their pupils, almost
all of whom were Jewish. Made to choose between Protestant and
Catholic schools, Jewish parents in Quebec opted for the Protestant
ones. In this absurd setting, my father learned to recite the poems
of Rudyard Kipling and to sing such imperial ditties as "On the
Road to Mandalay."

In the Montreal where my father grew up, invisible walls of
ethnic exclusiveness divided communities from one another. For
children in the city's Jewish ghetto, French Canadians were a distant and vaguely menacing presence. Anglo-Saxons were also
remote. My father had virtually no contact with non-Jews, apart

from his teachers, before he attended university. The first time he ever really talked to a non-Jewish girl was in the lineup to register for classes at McGill.

From the time he was six or seven, my father played the highly prized role of cantor at his father's weekly religious services. Although he was a rabbi, my grandfather earned his living as a "shochet," a butcher whose trade was the slaughter of cattle according to Jewish ritual. Most of the men in his flock were fellow shochets. My grandfather led them in prayer. In the Hasidic tradition, they linked arms and danced and sang. Religious worship and prayer were central to these gatherings, of course, but there was more to them than that. They functioned as a social club and a nascent trade union as well, where people who did the same unpleasant work in the abattoirs could share their joys and sorrows. At my grandfather's house, participants could feel completely at home in a strange land.

My grandfather's orthodoxy was leavened by the Hasidic emphasis on emotion. In this version of Judaism, the rabbi had to be charismatic, fired with the ability to touch his followers and to tap into their passions. Apparently my grandfather had what it took, with his powerful voice and intellect, and he looked the part with his long red beard. His circle of Jewish working men loved and admired him. If charisma generated joy and fulfilment, however, it could also foster anger and feelings of betrayal. Hasidic sects are given to splits, as one rabbi proclaims that his truth is the only way and denounces another for false teaching.

My grandfather — his name, Getzel, meant "little God" — was steeped in the ways of Hasidism long before he came to Canada. When he was seven or eight, his parents arranged for him to study with a rabbi. On weekdays, the boy journeyed from the tiny village where he lived to the nearby city of Czernowitz. On these odysseys to the huge, exciting world of the metropolis, my grandfather brought a lunch, which usually consisted of a little bread, cottage cheese and whey. The rabbi taught the boy to read and write Hebrew and directed his study of the Talmud.

When my grandfather was nine, his father, Mechel, took him to a celebration held by a Hasidic rebbe in a village not far away. (Such rebbes, in the Hasidic tradition, often inherited their positions and had not studied to become rabbis.) The impressionable young boy stood in the midst of the large crowd that had gathered outside the rebbe's house in a driving downpour. When the rebbe and his family came out on a balcony with a canopy overhead, the crowd cheered. But my grandfather, one of my father's sisters proudly told me, wondered whether it was fair for the rebbe's son, about his age, to be sheltered from the rain while he was not. He would be stubborn in his insistence on fairness for the rest of his days.

My grandfather was only twenty when, with a baby son and a pregnant wife, he celebrated the start of a new century by setting off for the New World. He was driven partially by the desire to put himself beyond the reach of the Austrian emperor, who was always on the lookout for young men to conscript into his armed forces. It was not unknown for a potential conscript to cut off the index finger on his right hand to avoid military service. But my grandfather had more on his mind than his aversion to the army. He believed his hopes for himself and his family could best be realized in America. By accident, he ended up in Canada. One part of North America was much the same as another to my father's parents; they could just as easily have landed south of the border, as many of their relatives did. Not long after their arrival, my grandfather travelled to New York City in search of work. Finding none, he and his wife and son headed for the little city of Sherbrooke, Quebec, ninety miles east of Montreal.

It was a peculiar place to settle. There were almost no Jews in the city, which was then an English-speaking enclave in French-speaking Quebec. The original settlers were Loyalists who had fled the horrors of the American Revolution. In Sherbrooke, my grand-father set up shop as a shochet. In addition, he served as the town's chief rabbi and Hebrew teacher, not that he had much competition for these posts. He spoke no English, but he overcame this handi-cap by striking a deal with the local Irish bishop, who wanted to learn to read the Old Testament in Hebrew. They took turns teach-ing one another.

My grandparents and their growing family stuck it out for thir-teen years in Sherbrooke before moving to the Jewish ghetto in Montreal's St. Urbain district. My grandfather, who hated slaugh-tering cattle, made a brief foray into the cottage cheese business. This went nowhere, and he soon found himself back in the abattoir.

The ghetto, with its narrow, tightly packed three-storey houses, outfitted with distinctive outdoor wrought-iron staircases, lay to the east of Mount Royal. The house the family bought on Esplanade stared up at the mountain, which rose above the centre of the city. The huge Catholic cross atop it, visible from far away, was a symbol of the city's dominant religion. Some of the early Jewish migrants to the city had already made it to the posh English enclave of Westmount. The Bronfmans, who founded Seagrams, were the symbol of Jewish wealth in Montreal. During the 1920s, the glory years of Prohibition, the family made a fortune supplying whiskey to Americans.

As a child, my father often took the streetcar with his mother to the Montreal market, where she would buy a live chicken and some fresh fish. He wasn't fond of the way the chicken would poke its head out of the bag to look at him on the way back home. And he ended up hating fish for the rest of his life; fish was food for the poor, he thought. On these shopping trips, my grandmother poured out her resentments against the Bronfmans. She wouldn't have minded a few comforts herself, and she looked on her husband as a good man who had no idea how to make money.

At home, my grandfather devoted himself to the study of the Talmud. He was noted for his dogged devotion to religion and prayed for hours each day. Equipped with phylacteries and a prayer shawl, he would pace back and forth in the dining room, which was cluttered with his books and scribblings. He sometimes carried a crying baby in his arms as he completed the daily rituals. In the male-centred world of Hasidic orthodoxy, tending to a child while praying was considered a major concession to his wife and daughters.

My father was expected to follow in his father's footsteps. He was to train as a rabbi, become an eminent scholar. When he was ten, my grandfather took him to New York, where my father performed in front of an important New York rabbi, drawing rave reviews for his recitation of a lengthy biblical passage in Aramaic, the ancient language in which the scriptures were first written. In the stratified world of Jewish orthodoxy, impressing the New York rabbi was a big deal. Aunts and uncles often took me aside on our family visits to Montreal to tell me in a confidential whisper about my father's star turn. By the time he was in his early teens, my father was proudly thought by the members of his family to be the most promising rabbinical student in Montreal. What a rabbi he would have made. But it was not to be.

A thunderbolt struck — or so the family legend goes — and my father's life was changed forever. When he was fourteen, an acquaintance secretly slipped him a copy of Charles Darwin's *On the Origin of Species*. The book was followed by others on socialism, likely passed along by an older in-law. The forbidden fruit in these volumes proved irresistible. And if the Darwinian view of evolution was right, my father concluded, then the Orthodox Judaism he had been working so hard to master must be wrong. From accepting evolution to embracing socialism was not a difficult step. For one thing, socialism of one variety or another was the dominant political preference of most Montreal Jews at the time. My father's conversion was remarkably swift.

He hid his new ideology, though, not least because he was afraid of my grandfather. The rabbi with the red beard was possessed of a terrible temper. As a boy, my father had often taken to his heels when his father exploded in rage and chased him with fists clenched. The frightened son would dart outside and hightail it down the street to his sister Esther's house, where he sought refuge.

My father's version of events presented him as undergoing a smooth, almost instantaneous transformation. But why he broke with Judaism has never been entirely clear to me. Many teenagers have books thrust in front of them without their lives being changed. What hunger dwelt in my father to get him to read the first book, and then to want more? Something about his own father's world was leaving him cold, even though he had every expectation that he could look forward to an honoured place in it.

To some extent, the break with his father can be explained within the volatile ways of the Hasidic tradition. Even though the position of rebbe was often passed from father to son, there was a great deal of infighting as well. The instance of a son disagreeing with his father, and storming off on his own course, was common enough.

And my father's break, although a considerable one, by no means amounted to a rejection of everything for which his father stood. In his own way, my grandfather was a social activist. During the 1920s, he led a dramatic struggle on behalf of his fellow butchers against their employers. At the time, a power struggle had broken out over who was to control the slaughter of cattle for Jews in Montreal and how the spoils from that slaughter were to be distributed. Rabbis fought other rabbis for control, and the shochtim, who did the dirty work in the abattoirs, agitated for higher pay and better working conditions. It was a class war of a highly particular kind. In this charged atmosphere, my grandfather took the dramatic step of setting up his own group of shochtim to provide kosher meat. What followed was a series of court cases, in which my grandfather argued that, as a rabbi and a shochet himself, he was qualified to rule on what was kosher and non-kosher meat. The stakes were high. If he won, the rebel shochtim would be paid directly by independent butchers. This would cut the rabbis who represented the prominent and wealthy members of the Jewish community out of the picture. It was an audacious initiative that put my grandfather up against powerful, vested interests. His house became a centre for the bearded shochtim, who often dropped in on Saturday nights to sit around the dining room table and debate their conditions in the abattoirs, as well as their opinions on Judaism and everything else under the sun.

At sporadic intervals over many years, the shochtim went on strike to advance their cause. Their struggle continued until after my grandfather's death in April 1942. A resolution of sorts was finally reached when the shochtim created a union to represent them. But for many years preceding that, my grandfather paid a price for his leadership of the movement. His income suffered greatly as a result of the battle, which made life tougher in a household with many mouths to feed.

By the time my father broke from Judaism, he had long been a witness to his father's fight on behalf of the men who worked in the abattoirs. He shared his father's conviction in this class struggle. He had chosen sides, and he never changed his mind.

If the ultimate reasons for a person's transformation are often unfathomable, a partial explanation for my father's break was that he yearned to be a part of the wider society. In Montreal, that meant breaking out of the confining walls of the ghetto. My father was a child of the New World. Just as the children of countless immigrants see their parents as out-of-place people with irrelevant ideas, my father was coming to see his father that way.

But why the leap to a new faith, Communism? Why did my father not turn to the materialist ethic of making it in the New World, as so many others in his situation did? I have come to think he had a core need for faith as a compass, by which he could make sense of a disordered world. French Canadians, though in the minority in Canada, formed the majority in Montreal. The Anglo-Canadian elite was a privileged minority whose language was adopted by Jewish immigrants. People reacted to the pressures generated in Montreal in different ways. My father's way was to abandon one orthodoxy while holding on to the habit of orthodoxy itself. The new faith to which he was drawn, like the old one, was characterized by charismatic leaders, passion and joy, but also by bitterness, hatred and deep feelings of betrayal. In his long journey, my father would never stray outside the temperament of the Old Testament.

Soon the chance arose to put his new socialist thinking to work in a practical setting. My father was already a student at McGill University when the Quebec government levied fees for attendance at public high schools in the province. The cost, though only a few dollars a year, meant that a poor family with a large number of children could not afford to keep them all in school.

The kids at my father's old high school, almost all of whom were Jewish, went on strike. My father came back to Baron Byng High to take part in the struggle. On the picket lines, and in the bid to win others to the cause, he discovered that he could speak in public, that others were stirred when he spoke. He was suddenly alive to the idea that he could be a leader. He had practised long and hard as a cantor and as an able learner of scripture. Now that gruelling effort was paying off in a very different setting. Although the strikers did not force the government to change its policy in the end, the strike had shut the school down. And it gave youthful political agitators, my father among them, a heaven-sent opportunity to try out their stuff.

By all accounts, my father was a charismatic, attractive young man. Even though he was almost painfully thin, he had a natural, winning smile. He believed in himself. He never doubted the truth of his inner voice. His great strength, and terrible weakness, was his certainty that he could impose his way of thinking on the world, however initially resistant the world might prove to be. Whether he was speaking to one person or a crowd, he conveyed urgency and hope. Central to his well-being was the conviction that he knew how to change the world for the better.

In 1932, at the age of seventeen, my father became the first member of his family to attend university. This great opportunity came to him not because he was a better student than his sisters, but because he was a male. Without complaint, his sisters went out to work and contributed to the cost of his education. If they ever resented this discriminatory treatment, they never showed it.

My father attended McGill University at a time when a quota system required Jewish students seeking admission to have higher marks than others. At McGill, his burgeoning socialism soon took a materialist and Marxist turn. What started as a journey away from Orthodox Judaism evolved into an implacable atheism. Voltaire's anti-clerical cry "Écrasez l'infâme" became his lifelong watchword. He would clench his teeth as he said it, and you could feel the anger when he repeated Voltaire's invocation to crush the infamy of religion. My father's hatred for God, which always raised uneasy hackles on my superstitious neck, stemmed from his rage that so much of his childhood was stolen from him by his religious studies.

My father ended up in psychology once he discovered that he was rather too squeamish for medicine. But politics was his true love, and politics was very much in the air. By those Depression days, social democrats and Communists were already entrenched in vicious antagonism as each struggled for dominance within the Left.

Initially, my father was attracted to the social democrats, who were just then founding a new national party, the Co-operative Commonwealth Federation (CCF). Ironically, it was a supporter of the CCF, a McGill professor, who helped him to widen his knowledge of Marxism — which he would use to scorn social democracy for the rest of his life. What drove him toward the Communists was the rise of fascism in Europe. He was seventeen and a half when Hitler became chancellor of Germany on January 30, 1933. Stopping the Nazis became his passion, and the Communist Party was the only instrument he believed was up to the job. The CCFers, led by the pacifist former clergyman J.S. Woodsworth, seemed far too preoccupied with the isolated world of Canadian domestic politics.

The Communists had one thing more going for them. They were the self-proclaimed tribunes of the Bolshevik Revolution of 1917. As my father would tell me many times during my childhood, he saw the Bolshevik Revolution as the greatest event in human history, leaving even the French Revolution as a pale progenitor. The Bolshevik Revolution was a rebirth for humanity, in his eyes. It was the beginning of a movement in which, for the first time ever, the needs, desires and goals of the majority of the population would take centre stage. During the French Revolution, he told me, the masses acted to bring the capitalists to power. In the Bolshevik Revolution, they acted for themselves.

Armed with these heady ideas, buoyed by the certainties they promised, my father entered the fray of the thirties, with all its posturing and pageantry. The Party line for the Communists of the world was established in Moscow, and that line changed periodically. Sometimes the changes were dramatic. During my father's first days as a Communist, the Party was deeply hostile to social democrats, depicting them as "social fascists" in the sulphurous phrase of the time. Because of their betrayal of the working class, social democrats were hardly to be preferred to the Nazis and fascists themselves. This position played no small role in preventing German Communists and Social Democrats from making common cause against Hitler in the crucial months leading up to the Nazi accession to power.

After Hitler had been in power for two years, Party central in Moscow put out the word that the line had changed. Social democrats and others on the Left were no longer to be publicly reviled. Instead, Communists were to work with them to establish a united front against the fascists. Canadian Communists, my father among them, embraced the new policy and busied themselves seeking alliances with other progressive forces. Much later, I was to discover that the Communist outlook always ranges between these two polarities — a splendid disdain for the views of others and a desire to form opportunistic, short-term alliances. Both poles proceed from the same fundamental perspective: the Communists regard themselves as the essential, exclusive political vehicle through which humanity will reach a transformed and better world.

For a while, my father considered volunteering to fight on the side of the Republic during the Spanish Civil War, a cause that drew many young Canadians and Americans. But he decided to stay in Montreal to help build the united front the Communists were constructing. He had learned by then that he had a special talent for wooing idealistic young Christians to the Communist banner. The honing of this talent led him to my mother.

Five

THE GRANDFATHER I GOT TO KNOW

IN HER QUIETER WAY, my mother was as tough-minded a Communist as my father.

You might imagine that young Christians in the 1930s would be well inoculated against atheistic Bolshevism, but there you would be wrong. The Student Christian Movement (SCM), active on many university campuses, was a hotbed of radicalism. For SCMers, the holy grail was pursued by demystifying Christianity to discover the real man who had been Jesus and to analyze the revolutionary social movement he led. Members spent time studying the scriptural records that helped piece together the story of Christ and his early followers. The irony of the SCM is that it produced as many atheistic Communists as it did Christians.

Edna May Quentin, the daughter of a Methodist missionary who spent thirty-five years in China, was attracted to the SCM in her early twenties. Shy, self-absorbed and idealistic, she had graduated from the University of Toronto in history and English and had gone on to obtain a master's degree in social work. My mother was born in China during one of her parents' long sojourns in Sichuan Province. Her first language, taught to her by her nursemaid, was Mandarin. Until she was ten, my mother was kept at the mission and educated

By the time I knew my grandfather, he was living in retirement in North Toronto. He was a wonderful storyteller, and whenever the opportunity arose, I coaxed him to relate another of his many adventures. He would reach up the sleeve of his shirt with his hand and proclaim, "Let's see what I've got up here." The story was brought down from his sleeve while I waited in delicious anticipation.

Once he told me the tale of how he had to serve as a doctor as well as a preacher on his mission in China. A middle-aged man came to him one day with a highly swollen abdomen. It appeared he had dropsy. My grandfather decided he had to carry out a surgical procedure to drain the fluids. He took an old door and laid it down outside and asked the patient to lie down on this makeshift operating table. It was a warm day, and my grandfather felt he needed the light of the sun to do his job properly. As he understood it, the incision had to be made with a scalpel. He sterilized his instrument and then looked closely at the abdomen, which was so swollen he wasn't sure where to make the cut. By this point, the man on the door had become visibly agitated. My grandfather decided that he needed one more consultation with his "how-to" medical book inside the house. He quickly rechecked the diagram before steeling himself and walking back outside. There lay the makeshift operating table, but the patient was gone, never to be seen again.

Another time he reached up his sleeve, my grandfather found a tale of banditry. He was riding on a ramshackle bus in Sichuan Province when bandits attacked. Shots were fired, and the passengers on board huddled low in their seats. Suddenly, the driver slumped to the floor. The bus swerved and plunged off the road. My grandfather leapt forward, jumping into the driver's seat. He struggled with the steering wheel, managing to get the bus back on the road as bullets whistled around him. A moment later, the passengers were cheering as the bus made its escape. His "derring do" was revealed on other occasions, too. Once, my grandfather almost drowned when he dove into a swift-flowing river to save a man who had fallen into the water and didn't know how to swim.

In one dramatic case, diplomatic finesse was required. An important town in Sichuan, close to the location of my grandfather's mission, was the site of a power struggle during the 1920s. The main part of the town was fortified and held by one warlord. An aggressor placed this stronghold under assault. Known for his linguistic skills and his even-handedness, my grandfather was summoned to act as a mediator. He was escorted by one side down to the no man's land between the two armies. Under the sightline of the opposing troops, he crossed a small bridge to the other side; then he was led through narrow streets and winding passages past bastions and towers. After a tense scene involving the chief lieutenants of the two warlords, a deal was struck and the siege of the town was lifted.

My grandfather was a proselytizer. During his long career, he wrote several books and an indeterminate number of pamphlets. His first book, published in 1909 when his name was still A.P. Quirmbach, carries the lurid title *From Opium Fiend to Preacher.* Set in the province of Hupeh, on the Yangtze River, it tells the true story of Cheng Ting Chiah, who became addicted to opium after he lost his wealth and his wife died. "Brooding over his misery and seeking relief from his pain," Cheng developed an appetite for opium that "became insatiable." "It was a bitter, lonely life," my grandfather wrote. "He was a wreck of his former self—this broken-down, half-blind, decayed gentleman earning a pittance by the use of his powers of mind and speech that he might buy a pipeful of opium and forget his sorrows."

The narrative describes Cheng's salvation as he is won over to Christianity and, through the power of the gospel, is able to turn away from opium. Cheng and my grandfather go their separate ways only after the former addict has himself become a preacher devoted to spreading the gospel.

The second of my grandfather's books is called *A Taoist Pearl*. Published in 1928, after he had changed his name to Quentin, it also tells the true inspirational story of a convert to Christianity.

Siao Chi San, born in north-central Hupeh, began life well enough, becoming a farmer and having children with his wife. But he felt a spiritual emptiness inside him and yearned for some way to overcome it. After endless turmoil, he was drawn to Taoism, with its promise of immortality for its followers. Leaving his family and his material possessions, he departed from his home, never to return. On his travels, he lived a life of monasticism, celibacy and asceticism.

For twenty years, Siao struggled with the Taoist philosophy, but then he was drawn to Christianity by chance encounters with some missionaries. In the Christian gospel, he found a light that shone brighter than anything he had yet discovered. For a time, he lived with my grandfather and other Christian missionaries. He ended his life a saintly man whose thinking combined elements of Taoism and Christianity.

The protagonists in both of my grandfather's books were lost individuals who passed through a terrible time of struggle only to achieve eventual redemption. My grandfather never doubted that, in the gospel of Christianity, Cheng and Siao would find complete salvation. He believed that to be true for everyone on earth.

My grandfather's life in China tested the balance in him between dogma and the acceptance of differences. It was his mission to seek converts, and this he set out to do for more than three decades. But those he encountered in China won a subtle and lasting victory of their own. My grandfather could not help but feel that theirs was a brilliant civilization, one which had developed approaches to life and spirituality that merited profound respect. When he returned to Canada for good, he faced a test in his ability to accept differences that came from a source much closer to him personally. That source was his daughter, my mother.

My mother took my father to meet her parents at Christmastime 1939. Despite the worldliness of my mother's parents, the 120-pound Jewish boy was a challenge for them. As he sat at their large oak dining room table wolfing down the food prepared by their live-in maid, the Quentins could be forgiven if they did not picture him as an ideal mate for their daughter.

Revealing a flair for drama, my parents eloped the same month the Canadian government declared the Communist Party and fourteen related organizations illegal. It was June 1940, and my father was living underground. To stay out of the clutches of the Royal Canadian Mounted Police, my father had grown a moustache and dropped his name, Mendel Laxer, going instead under the alias Robert Owen. (Years later, when I learned that Robert Owen had been a famous nineteenth-century British socialist, I marvelled at the naïveté of my father's choice. On the other hand, Canadian police have never been particularly tuned in to broad cultural currents. In 1970, a Montreal acquaintance of mine whose apartment was searched during the War Measures Act crisis had his books on cubism seized. The police evidently thought they were on to a possible Havana connection.)

My father had good reason to make himself scarce. His older brother Max, whom he had converted to Communism, had been arrested in 1940 and interned at Petawawa in Canada's version of a concentration camp. Max was locked up for a year with fellow Communists and others hardly to his taste, German and Italian fascist sympathizers who had also been rounded up by the authorities. About a hundred leading Communist activists were interned in camps. No charges were laid against them, and none was allowed a trial.

In these dire circumstances, my father had no income. He lived with my mother in her Toronto apartment on the few dollars a week she earned as a social worker for the YWCA. My parents' wedding,

· in Bradford, Pennsylvania, fell on the very day that Marshal Pétain signed the armistice with Germany, ending the French army's resistance to the German invasion. Neither the Laxers in Montreal nor the Quentins in Toronto were told about the marriage.

The secret wedding was both romantic and eminently practical. By the time of their elopement, my parents were already adept at cloaking their relationship. On one occasion not long before the wedding, my parents were at home in my mother's apartment when her brother Peter unexpectedly dropped in for a visit. My father scrambled into a closet and hid behind a pile of clothes. While my mother stood with her heart in her mouth, Peter opened the closet door and hung his jacket inside. He stayed for an hour or so without discovering the revolutionary from Montreal lurking behind his sister's wardrobe.

My parents' marriage was kept from my mother's family until the summer of 1941. The first to learn of it was my mother's sister Margaret, by then a medical doctor. My mother arrived at the family home to inform her horrified sister that she thought she was having a miscarriage. Luckily, my grandparents were out of town. As Margaret put her pregnant sister to bed, she was somewhat mollified to learn that my mother was married, even if it was to a Jewish Communist. During the bleeding my mother experienced that night, it is possible that I lost a twin.

My grandmother was brittle about the unwelcome news. She must have bristled at the thought she had been lied to even about her son-in-law's name. At the first opportunity, she told my mother in an accusing tone, "You've made your bed, and now you must lie in it." But a few days later, my grandmother had a change of heart. She telephoned my father and offered an olive branch. "I'd like you to call me Mother," she told him. Stilted it was, but the gesture worked. From then on, my father always felt my grandmother accepted him.

My grandfather took the news of the marriage with good grace. He would not have chosen my father as the man for his daughter, but right from the start there was an easy chemistry between them. It helped that my father did not mind being welcomed by the members of an upper-class WASP family. In later years, I often saw my grandfather and my father seated together in the big living room chatting intimately about politics, history and philosophy. When he was with my mother's parents, my father adopted a live-and-let-live tone that was very uncharacteristic. It didn't hurt when my grandfather reciprocated by telling my father how much he respected Tim Buck, the leader of Canada's Communists.

My grandparents' acceptance of my father improved my mother's relationship with her parents as well. Past tensions between them melted away.

Etiquette and manners were heavily emphasized by my grandmother and Aunt Margaret. At the beginning of a meal, you had to say the blessing "O Lord of good, come bless this food...in Jesus' name, Amen." You were never to allow your elbow to rest on the table, although forearms were permitted. "Please" and "thank you" were mandatory wherever appropriate. The word "what" was verboten if you didn't hear what someone said; you had to say "pardon me," especially to adults. Before you left the dining room table at the end of a meal, you had to ask to be excused. And Grandma and Aunt Margaret were offended almost to insensibility if you ever pointed at anything. Even if you were walking down the street with them and wanted them to see a bird in a tree, you had to keep your arms perfectly still and describe precisely where they could look for it.

I didn't really get to know Uncle Peter as I was growing up — during my childhood he was an executive of a chemical company based in Asia and South America. But Aunt Margaret played a large role in our lives. Although she was a conservative who took formalities very seriously, Margaret was an extraordinarily accomplished and independent woman. She had finished a degree in household economics at the University of Toronto at the beginning of the thirties before going on to medical school and becoming a doctor. After that she studied paediatrics, spending more than ten years in all at university. During the war, she joined the Canadian army, serving as a doctor in the forces. When she was discharged, Margaret set her course for life. She would practise paediatrics, remain single and live in the home of her parents.

Whenever my siblings and I were sick, Margaret came to Melita Street to see us, carrying her black bag. She would place her cool fingers on our fevered brows and tell us to take deep breaths as she checked us out with her stethoscope. She was our medicare in the fifties, providing us with free and unlimited treatment. When I came down with the measles at the age of six, she drove me up to the big house in North Toronto and installed me in a bedroom on the second floor. It was several days before my fever broke and she took me home.

Despite her kindness, my brother and sister and I were a little afraid of our aunt. We made up a game we called "Margaret"; the person who was "It" had to play Margaret, jumping from chair to chair and sofa to sofa in the living room without touching the floor. Those being pursued could move freely. When you were caught, you had to take a turn as Margaret.

My siblings and I often stayed at our grandparents' house. If I was there on a weekend, I went with them to church, sitting through the adult service with my grandparents and Aunt Margaret at Deer Park United. I loved the atmosphere of the great quiet church with its elegant pillars, its stained-glass windows and its slightly musty odour. Standing to sing the hymns was particularly enjoyable. Fervent, tuneful hymns were real moments of passion for these rather repressed Protestants. Sermons were more to be endured. Dr. Russell, who had been the minister at Deer Park since Jesus was crucified, it seemed to me, would start off well with some sort of tough question for the parishioners: "Are we truly our brothers' keepers?" or "What do we owe the poor?" This would be followed by lengthy quotations from scripture that seemed rather tangential to the question at issue. If it was a sunny morning and light was streaming down through the great, high windows, you could nod off a little as you watched the bits of dust floating in the shafts of sunshine. By then, thoughts were turning to the delicious dinner to come. Images of tender roast beef, mashed potatoes and creamy cauliflower filled my mind. But what really made me salivate were thoughts of the gravy boat, the side dish full of an assortment of pickles and the special relish that came in its own small serving bowl.

Sunday dinner at my grandparents' was a sumptuous affair with formal place settings and courses carried in on silver platters and fine china. Grandpa and Grandma sat at the head and foot of the table. Edith, their rather frail maid, who was over seventy, was summoned to carry in the next course from the kitchen whenever Aunt Margaret rang a tiny silver bell. Edith herself ate in the huge kitchen, which overlooked the backyard. Stairs connected her quarters on the second floor, at the back of the house, to a hall beside the kitchen. It bugged me that my grandparents had a maid. I didn't mind the luxury of their house, but ringing a bell for someone and then scolding her for not doing this or that made my skin crawl.

Conversation at these dinners was always rather formal. People told each other how nice they looked and commented on the weather. The other perennial topic was traffic accidents. News about a spectacular car crash was inevitably followed by barely audible exclamations of "Oh, dear." There were long periods when the only sound was the quiet clicking of knife and fork. Margaret made irritable comments about how Edith was handling a particular dish. Sometimes she rushed out to the kitchen to provide more instructions. If my father was present, he would clear his throat and ask in an innocent tone, "How was Dr. Russell's sermon?" "It was really fine, a lot to think about," Margaret would reply. Uncle Bill, who was married to my mother's younger sister, Julia, would add sonorously, "Dr. Russell's sermons are so well crafted." Having trapped them, my father would ask what Dr. Russell had *said* in his sermon. This led to awkward silences as people tried to remember just what the reverend had talked about.

Despite all the training I'd received in proper etiquette, I once made a major faux pas after dinner. I was sitting on the living room floor, leafing carelessly through the newspaper, when I saw a picture that drew my attention. "Who's that fathead?" I asked my grandmother. "Why, dear," she replied in shock, "that's Dr. Russell."

Having been taught the virtues of atheistic Communism, I naturally regarded my grandparents' religion as full of pious sentiments that couldn't be trusted. However, I had a more kindly disposition toward God than did my father, who regarded the Almighty as a ruling-class stooge. I wasn't sure I was an atheist, though, a thought I kept to myself. After all, I had been taught that the universe was infinitely large and had existed forever. How did it get there, I wondered, if there was no God? But if God created it, who created God? I was afraid of death, which I thought about a great deal, so the idea of an afterlife seemed attractive. But the kind of afterlife my grandparents seemed to have in mind, involving constant singing in a holy pale light by the side of God and Jesus, sounded dull.

One summer, my grandmother and Aunt Margaret took me, along with the redoubtable Aunt Jean, to see Shakespeare's *The Merchant of Venice* at the Stratford Festival. We stayed in a fussy little inn and lunched at a golf and country club on the edge of town, where the specialty was a creamy potato salad garnished with bits of green. In the company of my tony WASP family, the play made me squirm.

My Toronto relatives were not overtly anti-Semitic, although from time to time they made remarks about Catholics. While carving the turkey at Christmas, my grandfather liked to comment on the part of the bird known as the pope's nose. And they all joked about the full-body baptisms conducted by some of the wilder Protestant sects, the punchline always being about a minister losing a convert beneath the waves. In front of me, though, they never said anything negative about Jews. What they exuded instead was a serene superiority. It was clear they felt that to be Anglo-Saxon was to be at the pinnacle of the human race. Each year on May 24, Queen Victoria's birthday, my grandmother hung a huge Union Jack down the front of their house. Grandma and Grandpa and Aunt Margaret knew in their bones that British was best.

While I could play the WASP to perfection in the way I spoke and in my mannerly behaviour with adults, there was some kind of barrier that I could never get past. Inside me, there was a rhythm and a temperature that felt different. With my mother's family, I was always aware of playing a role.

My instinct was to hedge my bets where religion was concerned. How could it hurt, I thought, to keep the door a little open? For a time Gord and I, along with other kids on Melita Street, attended Sunday school at a United church not far from our house. My parents had no problem with this; my father considered the Bible part of our society's cultural heritage, and he believed everyone should be familiar with it. In the church's small basement, we memorized the Ten Commandments and heard the stories of the Old Testament and the New. The tales were full of life and action, and I especially loved the Christmas story of the baby Jesus coming to save a sinful world. I hated Easter, though; the idea of Jesus proceeding toward Jerusalem, where he knew he would be betrayed and crucified, bothered me greatly. I detested the part of the story in which he was nailed onto the cross, and I was not comforted by his resurrection. I was completely unconvinced that Jesus actually rose from the dead. In my personal version of Christianity, the world was saved by the birth of the Christ child, not by the grisly nightmare of Good Friday and Easter.

Easter also made me uneasy because the idea that the Jews killed Christ was prevalent among other kids. I'm not sure where they got that idea, but it passed through the popular grapevine like nursery rhymes and children's games. On the playgrounds and hockey rinks, there was a strong undercurrent of anti-Semitism that Easter seemed to provoke. Lots of kids thought of Jews as moneylenders, too, and somehow they had heard of Shylock. It all fit together in the culture of the street.

During the Easter holidays, my parents would often take us to Montreal to spend a few days with my father's relatives. It was good to be brought under the warm cloak of their affection at that time of year. When we reached Kingston, the halfway point on the train ride, we would remark to one another that it was time to drop our WASP identity and put our Jewish side on display.

Hanging out with my cousins was wonderful. Playing road hockey felt especially right in the home of the Montreal Canadiens and Rocket Richard. My family usually stayed with Uncle Max, then known mostly as Jack. During our visit we would circulate from the home of one aunt and uncle to the next, in a whirr of parties that never ended. The parties were flavoured by the lipstick of aging aunts, which you had to wipe off your cheek after you had been kissed, and the odour of the cigars smoked by uncles busy downing glasses of neat Scotch. There was never a pause in the laughter and conversation. At the beginning of such gatherings, various uncles would come up slyly and stuff folding money into one of my pockets. I never counted it, since I knew it was really for my father. The bills were to supplement the fifty dollars a weeks the Party paid him. My father had helped recruit some of these uncles and aunts as Party members, and often he would gather a coterie of his sisters, his brother Jack and a few of the in-laws around him for a political chat. He would hold forth on the world situation and the work of the Party, and he would hear in turn what his relatives had to say about the dark situation in Quebec because of Duplessis and the Padlock Act. My father's mother was old and bent, a little scary-looking. She would embrace me and say a few affectionate words in her strongly accented English, but I always felt ill at ease with her and was eager to go and play with my cousins.

Through these relatives, I had my connection to the early days of my father's family in Canada. The same stories were lovingly recounted during every visit to Montreal, and the best storyteller of them all was my father's sister Dora. Married to a doctor, Dora lived in a big, comfortable house in Outremont. She had a fine-featured, slightly beak-shaped face, expressive eyes and hunched shoulders. She was a denizen of her large kitchen, presiding over it from the early hours of the morning until late at night. We hung out there while she cooked potato latkes, or even bacon in her wicked moments. The world she recreated was a world of odd characters, each striving in his or her own way to make a go of life in a strange new country. When she and my father were growing up, their family lived next to a collection of cousins and aunts and uncles. On the first floor of the house next door was a big barrel stuffed with clothing for cousins of both genders. In the morning girls and boys would search the barrel for shirts, socks, dresses or pants. If they were lucky, the clothes actually fit.

Aunt Dora loved to tell tales of the personalities in our extended family. There was the aging aunt who refused to get out of bed for seven years. There was an uncle everyone called Willie who had owned a car, a comparative rarity in the Montreal of the early twenties. Willie was noted for his contrariness, and his specialty was to drive fast in the city and very slowly on what passed for highways in Quebec in those days. Once, when crossing the border into New York State, Willie answered the immigration official's question "Where were you born?" with the sly retort "Tuchus, Quebec." His hunch that the Yiddish for "rear end" would pass for a French place name proved correct, and he was waved across the border.

Border crossings were a big deal to the Jews of Montreal, many of whom had relatives in the U.S. Then, as later, New York was a mecca for Canadian Jews. In the twenties, many Jews taking the train to the big city attempted to smuggle live chickens across the border. The chickens were sometimes kept in boxes or bags that were stowed in the spaces between one rail car and the next. People were always getting out of their seats for mysterious little trips to check on the chickens. Between the cars they met other people doing the same thing. Stories of U.S. immigration personnel walking through the passenger cars, while muffled chicken-clucking could be heard in the background, were favourites at family gatherings.

One character who always came up in Aunt Dora's stories was the great-uncle who maintained a shadowy existence in the wool business, running a store in Montreal's French-speaking east end. When he moved the store from one location to another, he put a sign in English in the window that read: "It's here, the wool store." Noted for his disputatious insistence on being right, he once had a disagreement with a relative about where a particular town was located. When they checked the map, which agreed with the relative, the great-uncle muttered that the map was wrong. Asked by a policeman to explain how it was that his car had hit the side of a bridge, he countered that the bridge had moved.

One summer, as Aunt Dora was fond of telling us, one of my father's sisters and her husband had the entrepreneurial impulse to open a summer resort. They rented a dilapidated old hotel north of Montreal at a place called La Macaza. An unpleasant little river flowed swiftly past the property. Their hope was that Jewish Montrealers would flock from the hot city to enjoy cool evenings, good cooking and swims in the frigid stream. But only the odd customer found the attractions of La Macaza irresistible, and the summer was spent with my father's relatives cooking for each other and lamenting that they had not discovered a local version of the Catskills.

In the 1920s, members of Montreal's Jewish community displayed the unmistakable idiosyncrasies of those who have been recently urbanized. When he was ten years old, my father broke his leg one day while playing on the street. As Aunt Dora loved to tell us, when he was carried back home, my father's sisters and mother insisted that he needed to take a laxative before he received medical treatment. Moving the bowels was exalted in the virtues of the ghetto.

Inevitably, I suppose, one of my father's sisters had married a man who was in the shmatte business. Periodically, Aunt Dora told us, this uncle would cut large pieces of fabric into odd-shaped remnants, which he would then sell to bargain hunters for more money than it would have cost them to buy the material in its original form. Another of my father's brothers-in-law had obtained an M.A. in mathematics and hoped for a career in the public service as a statistician. The Depression shattered any chance of such employment. Instead, the brother-in-law, whose name was Sam, founded a bridge club, which he and my father's sister were to run for eons. Sam became a legendary figure, credited by many as the creator of bridge as a serious pastime in Canada. Whenever we saw my aging uncle, he was padding around his downtown Montreal apartment, always dressed in a suit, always with a cigar in his mouth, and always about to depart for the bridge club.

Malka, one of my father's sisters, had moved to New York and gotten a job at Macy's. Before setting out, she had already met and married Louis, a Jewish immigrant from the cockney east end of London. Louis, a skilled metallurgist who did all kinds of jobs during his decades in New York, including sign-painting, had a volcanic temper. Even in his sixties, he had calmed only a little. In restaurants, he almost always sent the food back, attacking the waiter in his cockney–New York accent as a calculating, cunning little so-and-so. I enjoyed trying to provoke Uncle Louis at family gatherings so that I could watch his bald head turn red, the warning sign that he was about to burst into a string of epithets.

But despite the stories and the warmth and the sense of connection these visits to Montreal gave me, I knew I wasn't Jewish. I loved my cousins, but I didn't make the grade as a Jewish kid. For one thing, all the Yiddish jokes had to be translated for me; since many of them turned on puns, the jokes were never quite the same in English. More importantly, my mother always felt that my father's sisters didn't accept her. She was just a "shiksa" to them, she would complain during the train ride back home, drawing on some remark or another as an example. I was acutely annoyed by her comments, but they had their effect. They brought me back to the world I lived in, the world that she and my father had designed for me, the world in which I was not supposed to be Jewish.

Seven

THE PLACID FIFTIES

ONE WARM SPRING AFTERNOON, I was out playing on Christie Street, a couple of blocks from home. Other kids were on their front porches, skipping rope on the sidewalk, throwing balls. Women made their way to and from the corner grocery store.

I happened upon Kathleen, a wiry girl who was in my class at school. We started talking, and she was standing very close to me when I said something that rubbed her the wrong way. Instantly, I faced a blur of well-aimed punches. I staggered and went down. Kathleen leapt on top of me, punching me with one hand and using her other to bang my head on the sidewalk. When she'd had enough she got up and casually walked away.

It was a classic kids' fight of the time. Being beaten up by a girl was humiliating, but the many kids and adults who were around when it happened didn't pay the slightest attention. When it was over, I climbed to my feet and slunk off home.

Fights at recess at McMurrich were as common as playing marbles, which we called "alleys." Indeed, many a fight was triggered when kids fell out over who had won in a game of alleys. As long as the combatants stayed discreetly in a corner of the schoolyard, the teachers on duty didn't bother to break them up. The yard on the lower side of the school was full of black stones with jagged edges. The stones were right to hand, ideal projectiles, and we often fired them through the air, starting fights when we hit someone.

Things got worse when gangs of boys, and sometimes girls, picked on one kid or a group of kids. Fights broke out on the way to and from school. Since everyone went home for lunch, there were four trips a day. Some tough boys would terrorize the same kids repeatedly. On occasion, kids were threatened with a beating unless they paid five or ten cents to pass unmolested.

Since the kids on Melita Street had farther to go to McMurrich than anyone else, we were subject to frequent alarums and attacks along the way. If we went to school by heading north first, then west, we ran into the Frew gang. If we went west first and then north, we ran into the Dewans. Both families had three or four boys in them, whose friends rounded out their retinues.

To get safely past these two family gangs, we formed a gang of our own. And we went them one better: we put together what we called an army. Even though I was small and not very tough — my main combat weapon was an ability to run away — I had picked up a few tactical pointers in previous encounters. I was also reading a lot about the adventurers of the American West, and my hero was a guy named Jim Bridger, famed for his exploits in the years before the Civil War.

I called together my brother and my friend Glenny from across the street to talk over the idea of an army. We huddled under the stairs that ran down from the second floor of our house into the little backyard. Gord and I had built a hideaway there, nailing bits of wood onto the staircase. We sat on the bare ground and hatched a plan, and decided to call our army BR, after Jim Bridger.

We made a flag with the device "BR" on it. Both girls and boys would be allowed to join. The army's ranks began with private and went on up from there to general. Having launched the whole thing,

I saw no reason not to appoint myself general, although I took care to appoint Glenny to the same exalted position. In the event of unrest in the ranks, it would be better to have two generals, not just one. Glenny was not a big guy either, but he was tough. Even better, he was quiet and not interested in taking over control of the army. With Glenny aboard, I recruited two other kids who lived across the street, Gordy and his little sister Wendy. Gordy didn't turn out to be much of a fighter, though; he would run home at the first sign of battle. Yet that was also my main strategy, so I figured he was okay. I also talked Alex, who lived down the block, into joining, although he was a thoughtful fellow who loved to collect things and didn't have much use for fighting. My mother insisted that we let Linda try out for the army too. She was only five, so we devised a simple recruitment test for her. She had to climb a wooden fence in the back lane. After she successfully struggled over it, she was admitted as a private. Brother Gord had the rank of captain.

Soon we had recruited fifteen or sixteen kids, most of them boys from Melita Street. It was rather an absurd little army, composed mainly of gentle types who amounted to anything resembling a force only when banded together in superior numbers. That didn't cramp our style, though. We divided the army into two units and spent many hours drilling and staging practice battles against each other. We fought them in the lane that ran behind the garages on one side of our street. Our weapons were the stones that sprinkled the parking areas behind houses where garages had been torn down.

The practice fights were brutal enough, and fun. Filling our hands with a goodly supply of stones, the two units began at opposite ends of the lane and clashed in the middle. We had only one tactic, but it was effective. Each unit was divided in two. One group advanced along the sides of the lane, from garage to garage. The other group provided cover by firing rocks overhead at the enemy.

Once the covering group had come alongside the first group, the first group leapfrogged ahead, receiving cover from the others. Usually one of the units routed the other and drove its members out of the lane.

Once the army was organized and trained, it was time to try it out against a *real* enemy. We picked the Frews, who lived in a house at the bottom of a hill a couple of streets north. Right next to their house was a huge advertising billboard. Behind the billboard — and this is what attracted us — was a tangle of paths, trees, bushes and long grass. There were also plenty of loose clumps of earth and stones. One Saturday afternoon, we marched up Christie Street with the BR flag snapping in the wind. We circled past the Frews' house and climbed the hill to attack from above. Each of us — we lost a few younger stragglers who were not allowed to cross Davenport Road, the major intersection on the way — was carrying handfuls of stones, and our pockets were similarly stuffed.

Both of our units crept down from the top of the hill. Then we stopped and planted our flag in the mud. We sent one unit, six guys, on ahead. When they caught sight of the Frews behind their house, they opened fire with a volley of rocks. Delighted by the challenge, the Frews dove into the trees behind the billboard and hurled rocks and hunks of earth back up the hill at us. The Frews climbed quite close to our advance unit, but a furious volley of stones drove them back again. After about ten minutes, we pulled back in orderly fashion, flag in hand, and retired over the top of the hill. It had been a splendid baptism of fire for the army. There would be other fights with the Frews over the next few years, all of them started in exactly the same way. During one retreat, Gord fell and cut his head and lay on the ground feeling faint. A woman came out of a neighbouring house and told the rest of us to scat. But she took Gord in and ministered to him, serving him tea and cookies before sending him on his way.

The army brought peace of a kind to the kids on Melita Street, although it was an armed peace, and there were many uprisings along the way. It was not that we were fighting less, but we were doing it in a more organized fashion. The army's sway extended to the next street north, and soon we had achieved a kind of security in our immediate neighbourhood.

On a number of occasions we mobilized the army for the journeys to and from school. We moved in a V formation with one unit on each side of the street, on the lookout for potential foes. A new threat arose after a year or two — Italians. Melita Street had been completely English-speaking when my family moved there, but that was beginning to change. The Italian kids stuck together and spoke to each other in a language we didn't understand. They didn't respond to the usually successful combination of threats and blandishments to join our army. Fighting broke out with a group led by a charismatic guy named Tony. After a desultory exchange of rocks and some hand-to-hand fighting in the lane, Tony and I met face to face and reached an uneasy truce.

An alternative to fighting in our neighbourhood was playing pranks on adults. Knocking on people's doors and then running away was a favourite, known to us as "nickey nickey nine doors." Usually this prank was carried out on warm summer evenings, but there was a winter variant that was even more obnoxious. One kid would knock on a door, and when it opened, the homeowner was pelted with snowballs. This prank was once raised to a higher level by leaning a Christmas tree against someone's front door. The door knocker was struck, and when the homeowner answered, he or she was hit by snowballs as well as the Christmas tree. Adults then were much less hesitant about scolding or even hitting someone else's child, and one neighbourhood father chased me down the street and right through the first floor of Lambert Lodge, the old folks' home a few blocks away that I had run into to throw him off the track.

Another favourite winter activity was freezing snowballs after soaking them in water, so that they became lethal. For some reason, we got into the habit of firing frozen snowballs at a delivery truck with the name Bacon on the door that was often in the neighbourhood. The driver became more and more exasperated. One day, about five of us were in the park on top of the hill when we saw Bacon stop his truck right below us. It was a perfect target. We rained a shower of snowballs down on the roof of the truck, enjoying the metallic clang that resulted.

The next thing we knew, Bacon was back in his truck and racing up the side street next to the park. A moment later, he was out of the truck and running at us. We took off, heading for our school. Bacon kept chasing us, and he was getting closer. In the nick of time, we found a passageway that was perfect for us but too narrow for Bacon, and we left him behind.

Not all of our activities were so antisocial. Although the kids in our neighbourhood rarely took lessons outside of school, my brother and I decided one winter to learn how to play Spanish guitar. After my mother rented guitars for us, Gord and I took the streetcar to the guitar teacher's little office. Visions of careers as musicians began to dance in our heads.

After three lessons, however, our careers were cut short by a transit strike. We never saw our guitar teacher again, but Gord and I thought we had learned enough to display our talents. We took our guitars to Lambert Lodge, walking right in the front door and upstairs to an alcove where a dozen residents were sitting around in armchairs. An elderly woman who spotted our guitars asked us to play something for them. Gord and I sat down as the group turned expectantly, waiting for the music. We knew how to pluck out the rudiments of one or two tunes, but you had to listen with a generous heart to recognize them. The women were kind, some of them saying how lovely we were. The men were not so polite. One of them remarked in disgust: "They don't even know how to play the guitar."

On Sunday evenings in the summer, the kids on Melita Street went down to the Union Carbide plant at the end of our block to watch the men from the plant play softball against other teams. We spent a little time playing softball and touch football ourselves, but our great love was hockey. Hockey was the game of games, and we played it from early autumn until well into the spring. We played it so much it was like life itself.

Because it was a dead-end street, Melita was perfect for road hockey. For goal posts we used horse manure or rubber boots, and for goalie practice we set up metal garbage cans at the side of the road. We played long after it grew dark, setting up our garbage cans under a street lamp.

The early 1950s was the golden age of natural ice rinks in Toronto. Christie Pits, just half a mile away, had four hockey rinks side by side. You could pick your own level of competition, and everyone knew the drill. To start a game, everybody threw their sticks down at centre ice. Then one participant threw half the sticks toward one end of the rink and the rest toward the other. That settled the teams. Late arrivals were slotted in as the game progressed. You could play till you dropped, which is what we did when the ice was right.

My hero was Rocket Richard of the Montreal Canadiens. The Canadiens were my team, too; a kid in the neighbourhood had convinced me that they were far more exciting than the Toronto Maple Leafs. Everyone's ultimate player in those days was either the Rocket or Detroit's Gordie Howe, and the ultimate showdown came whenever the Canadiens played the Red Wings in the Stanley Cup finals. It was the age of Foster Hewitt and radio; nothing equalled the tingling drama of his voice as you curled up on a chesterfield and listened to the game on Saturday nights.

On Sunday afternoons, Gord and I and a couple of friends went to Junior A hockey games at Maple Leaf Gardens. We would walk along the railway tracks for close to a mile, and then through the downtown streets from there. For fifty cents, we could see a double-header, one game with the Toronto Marlies, the other with St. Michael's Majors. About five thousand people turned out for each of the games, twice as many when the Junior Canadiens, starring Henri Richard, "the Pocket Rocket," came to town.

The Leafs always played the Canadiens over the Christmas holidays on a Wednesday night at Maple Leaf Gardens. Two days before the game, the Gardens would put a few hundred tickets on sale; the rest of the building went to season-ticket holders. Gord and I would set our alarm clock to go off at 5:30 a.m., and we were always the very first people there when we arrived at six. The cleaners let us come inside to sit under the ticket wicket until it opened three hours later. By then, the line stretched all the way along the hall of the Gardens.

Gord and I bought our tickets with money earned from our paper route. We always got an extra one for Uncle Bill, who was happy to take us to the game. Our tickets put us high up in the greys, at the very top of the stadium, but it was a thrill to see our heroes, especially the Rocket, on the ice.

Melita Street had many wonderful adventures to offer, but danger and even tragedy were never far away. Death and disease were also the stuff of life in our neighbourhood, as I was to learn.

Tragedy struck the home of our next-door neighbours when fourteen-year-old Georgie B. went to work for the local butcher and proceeded to cut his right hand off in the bacon-slicing machine. Mrs. B. spent most of the next few days at the hospital, but when she was home she sat on her front porch crying with her head in her hands. My mother went over to her house, something she almost never did, making Mrs. B. cups of tea and trying to cheer her up about her son's future. In the evenings, when Mr. B. got home from work, he sat out on the porch looking listless, barely turning his head in the direction of his distraught wife.

Georgie dropped out of school not long after the accident. It put him out of commission for a few months, but when he turned sixteen he learned how to drive a truck with his left hand, using his right arm to shift gears. He found occasional work doing that. During his spare time, he began collecting carrier pigeons. He assembled cages for the birds and put them out back on a narrow stretch of roof over the first floor of the B. house. We had a similar bit of roof on our house, and I would go out there to watch Georgie take out his pigeons, hold them on the stub of his handless arm and send them off on flights from which they soon returned.

Georgie B.'s tragedy was far from unique on Melita Street. Next door to us on the other side lived a family with four sons. One summer, when three of the brothers went for a swim alongside a rowboat in Lake Simcoe, the youngest one, about my age, disappeared beneath the waves and drowned. Two other boys from Melita Street also drowned during those years. Two doors down from us, a boy of my age developed tuberculosis and was sent to a sanatorium for two years.

My friend Gordy's sister Wendy, one of our first army recruits, came down with polio one August. As a consequence, the growth in one of her legs was stunted. In those days before the polio vaccine, there was terror every year in late summer, just around the time of the annual Canadian National Exhibition. My parents tried to keep Gord and Linda and me out of crowds during the most dangerous weeks, and we often spent them visiting my mother's parents in Muskoka.

Once a week, my brother and I paid the bill for our paper route to our boss, Mr. Weeks, who maintained an office of sorts in a garage about a mile from our house. His desk was a flat slab of wood resting on four high metal cans. Mr. Weeks was an overweight man in his sixties with a large pinkish face, a gash of white hair and a violent temper. All of the carriers were afraid of him. If you were a little late in paying your bill, he would phone you at home and order you to appear before him, cash in hand. He was always waiting with a snarl.

One day another carrier told me that Mr. Weeks was mad at me. I lived in apprehension of what might be in store for several days. The dreaded time came, and I turned into the lane and proceeded to the garage. Inside was a man I had never seen before. "Where is Mr. Weeks?" I asked. "Mr. Weeks died yesterday," said the man behind the table. What a relief, I thought—and then I felt horrible. I never found out what Mr. Weeks had been angry about.

Early television shows like *Father Knows Best* and *Ozzie and Harriet* promoted the idea that the fifties was an uncomplicated decade. People were prosperous and reassuringly normal. Crime and violence were minimal. The two-parent family, a haven of safety and calm, was alive and well. But the stereotype was not borne out on Melita Street. Day after day, the front pages of the newspapers I delivered were full of stories about murder, rape, sensational bank robberies and threats by the Americans and the Soviets to use atomic bombs against each other. Children were often in mortal danger. "Torture Boy, 2, Murder Charged," one banner headline read. And another: "Tries to Murder 2 Children, Father Kills Self with Knife."

Kids without organized activities were kids with a lot of time on their hands, and we were allowed to wander around on our own from a very young age. When I was nine, I was sexually abused on several occasions by a man in his early twenties in a laneway next to our street. I didn't know who he was, and I never told my parents anything about it.

It wasn't just strangers who posed a danger. Beside the lane on the other side of our street was a construction company that produced huge concrete blocks. When the company was shut down in the evenings and on weekends, my friends and I would climb those blocks high into the inside of the warehouse. If any of us had ever fallen from the top, we would have been seriously injured. Similarly, from the roof of our house, we had an eagle's view of the neighbourhood. The more daring of our friends would jump across the narrow alleyway to the next house and then back again. They'd have been lucky to survive a fall from that height.

The most treacherous place was the railway tracks. All through the neighbourhood, you could hear the hum of the trains going by. On our street, the houses would shake gently when a big freight train passed. A train whistle was a magnet drawing us to the tracks. We would climb between the boxcars, holding onto them for a brief ride as the engines were shunting them. You had to be careful, as you crawled across the track between the cars, that they were not about to be moved. There would be a sudden loud crunch as an engine pushed up against a string of cars. The whole line of cars would shudder, pause, then start to roll forward. Even very young kids, including my sister Linda, went to play on the tracks with their older brothers and sisters.

We kids survived on our own for much of the time. But there were moments when Melita Street was a place where everyone belonged. On long evenings during a midsummer heat wave, everybody sat out on friends' porches, the women in loose-fitting dresses, the men in undershirts. The kids congregated on someone's front lawn or took over the street.

Eight

MUSKOKA

PERCHED IN THE LIVING ROOM of our house on Melita Street, looking out the second-storey front window. Any moment my Aunt Margaret would drive down the street in my grandmother's perfectly maintained Pontiac. My suitcase was packed, and I was ready for adventure. Someone had told me that counting seconds would make time go by more quickly. I got to about twenty-five and decided that was even more boring. Instead, I focused on the excitement of the coming drive to Muskoka.

At last, the dark-blue car with its brilliant chrome bumpers came into view. At the curb, I said goodbye to my mother — she and my father, brother and sister would be joining us in a week — and climbed into the back seat. On the other side of the back seat, hidden behind a suitcase and a wicker basket, was my grandfather. He was hunched against a pillow and looked tired. At the wheel was Aunt Margaret, coolly competent as always, and beside her was my grandmother.

We were off on our annual holiday. Muskoka, a land of lakes, rocks and pines about a hundred miles north of Toronto, was the most perfect place in the world, as far as I was concerned. While I often imagined my grandfather at his mission in the mountains of China, Muskoka was where I knew him best. Every summer my grandparents and Aunt Margaret rented a cottage there, on one of the larger lakes. My favourite cottage was located on Lake Rosseau. It was much more than a cottage, actually. In the 1920s, the magnificent two-storey house, with its multitude of bedrooms and its huge old-fashioned kitchen, had been an inn. Down a slight hill from the long verandah was the L-shaped wharf, which jutted out into the lake.

The wharf had been built to handle the steamers that plied the Muskoka lakes. In the late nineteenth and early twentieth century, wealthy vacationers discovered Muskoka as an earthly paradise. In the summers, well-to-do Americans and Canadians took the train north to Gravenhurst at the southern tip of Lake Muskoka. There they boarded an elegant lake steamer, the *Sagamo*, with sleeping cabins and a dining room. Passengers were dropped off at inns and hotels along the way. At Port Carling, the town's swing bridge was wheeled to one side to allow the *Sagamo*, with its tall smokestacks, to pass through the lock and into Lake Rosseau. I slept in a cabin on the *Sagamo* once, as my family made passage across a foggy Lake Muskoka. Through the round cabin window I saw a ship going past us in the opposite direction, its blazing lights reverberating off the water and then melting into the fog. The summer I was ten, the *Sagamo* landed at our dock to drop someone off, though the days when it made regular trips were long in the past. I watched the vessel arc around an island as it set course to approach us, sounding its deep horn over the water.

It took ages for Aunt Margaret to drive us up Yonge Street to the outskirts of the city. Yonge Street, Highway 11, was the world's longest street, and it ran through all the towns along the route to Muskoka. I loved to see the various Main Streets with their general stores and barber shops. They were so unlike the downtown of the city where I lived. But I was restless by the time we rolled into Orillia several hours later. We always had lunch there in the large park where Lake Simcoe meets Lake Couchiching. Aunt Margaret would get out the steamer rug and the wicker picnic baskets, and we'd sit under the shady trees not far from a statue of Champlain, who had journeyed through this territory centuries earlier. She set out dishes, cutlery and linen napkins before unpacking the devilled eggs, finely cut sandwiches and salad. We sat and ate quite properly. Then there was a little time for me to run around the park, listen to the breeze rustling the dark green leaves, climb on the base of Champlain's statue, and go over to the shore to watch the sailboats and launches out on the water.

The trip to the cottage with my grandparents and Aunt Margaret conveyed me not merely to a new physical location but to a different spiritual space. By the end of lunch, I had crossed a boundary of the imagination into the world of my grandfather. He was the person who most gave me a physical sense of my own country, or at least the part of it where rocks, pines and lakes stretched on forever to the north. Back in the car for the remainder of the journey, I waited impatiently for the great grey granite rocks that signalled we were getting there. When we crossed the Severn River, the landscape altered abruptly, and we entered the land of the Canadian Shield, with its one million lakes. Half of Canada lies in the land of the shield. It was mid-afternoon when we arrived at the cottage on Lake Rosseau.

Beside the wharf at the Lake Rosseau cottage was a two-storey wooden boathouse that leaned a little rakishly to one side. Upstairs were living quarters. When my parents and siblings arrived, I moved down from the main house to stay with them. The single greatest charm of the boathouse was the toilet at the end of the long porch on the second floor. If no one was around you could safely sit there with the door wide open, enjoying a splendid view of the lake. Less charming was the daytime proclivity of bats to hide in the nooks and crannies of the boathouse, so that they could swoop overhead at night. My mother feared the little winged creatures and passed on to me the terror that they could become entangled in your hair.

On Saturday evenings, we gathered in the main house for a family dinner. Aunt Margaret fussed with the maid, Edith, who would have travelled to the cottage by bus, over every aspect of the meal. If my mother was present, she too was pressed into service. Aunt Margaret, while a very good cook, hated labour-saving devices, always believing that mind-numbing chores were the way of the Lord. She also had the rich person's aversion to anything that might deplete the family fortune. If she had you peeling potatoes, you were to remove only the thinnest of skins. One summer she had us carefully wash out all the cans left over from soups and vegetables. (Even good cooks used canned products back then.) She delivered the pristine cans to a man down the lake who had collected them as scrap in previous summers. But this summer, he was no longer in the scrap business. So, as Margaret informed us, he simply rowed the cans out into the lake and dumped them into the water.

After dinner we played canasta and waited for the Saturday night thunderstorm to develop. For some reason, there always was a violent, natural "son et lumière" show after our Saturday dinner. As the rain swept down and the lightning flashes edged closer, our little group grew tense. My grandfather was not perturbed, but the Quentin women, including my mother, were always agitated by thunderstorms.

The main house was at the bottom of a steep, tree-covered bluff, so there was always the possibility that a tree could be struck by lightning and then crash down on the roof. Lightning even struck the house itself a number of times. Once, a huge clap of thunder was accompanied by fuses blowing and sparks shooting out of the stove in the kitchen. Another time, when my sister was in an upstairs bathroom, light flashed from the water pipe. During the most violent phase of the storm, we were always made to sit in the middle of the living room, candles at the ready. No one was to cook, run water or take a bath. It was all great fun. One fresh Sunday morning after a storm, I found a tree that had been broken in half by lightning. I picked up a hand-sized splinter of wood to keep for good luck, on the assumption that lightning could not strike in the same place twice.

At the cottage on Lake Rosseau, my grandfather taught me how to row a boat, how to bait a fishing line and, most of all, how to catch bullfrogs. You had to be very determined to snag one. You'd sneak up behind a large frog as it lazed on the sand, its eyes bulging, the sacks at the side of its mouth swelling and shrinking. Then, with a sudden pounce, you snapped your hand down. If you hesitated or flinched, the frog leapt away. After my grandfather had shown me how it was done, I got pretty good at it, although I always let the frogs go afterward. Bullfrogs were too big to keep. A few times I kept small toads or little frogs in bottles, but they soon grew smelly and were not pleasant to have around. Once, on a hunt for bullfrogs by the edge of the lake, I stepped on a beehive. An angry swarm of bees chased me back to the house. Four bee stings later I was lying in my bed, with my grandfather comforting me about the ways of an imperfect world.

I spent hours in the lake perfecting my swimming, staying there until my lips turned blue. You had to wait exactly one hour after lunch before you could swim; otherwise, the wisdom of the day held, you would be stricken with a severe stomach cramp and would drown. When I wasn't swimming I was rowing the flat-bottomed punt along the shoreline below the great bluff. In my mind, every large tree jutting out above the little cove was in a place where pirates could have duelled. Every year a family named Jones with a boy about my age stayed nearby, and we spent afternoons acting out cowboy and detective adventures in the woods behind his cottage.

I felt completely at home with my grandparents and Aunt Margaret, but visiting relatives were a different story. Great-aunt Jean had a way of peering down her nose at everyone. So practised was she at this that she could tilt her head and look down on men who were considerably taller than she was. She belonged to a ladies' club in Toronto and was always telling everyone about the important and wealthy people she had seen there. When my grandmother referred once to Aunt Jean's "women's club," Jean corrected her haughtily. Another of Jean's favourite topics was her annual spring cruise from New York to Bermuda.

Great-aunt Jean looked down on everybody, so I never felt particularly singled out. But other aunts and uncles, well aware that my father was a Communist organizer, acted as though my siblings and I were riff-raff from the wrong side of the tracks. They did not say anything directly, but I had become something of an expert on how to read the people in the worlds in which I moved. I knew these relatives thought they were better than the members of my immediate family. We just weren't their kind of people.

The hierarchy in my grandmother's family was arranged in a fairly straightforward way. Because the Harrises didn't think my grandmother had done well to marry a penniless Methodist minister, Grandma, despite her ample means, was relegated to the lower reaches of her family. Those Harrises with seats on the Toronto Stock Exchange occupied the loftier heights, along with my Great-aunt Dolly, who married a wealthy American industrialist. Sometimes Dolly's son would visit, roaring up from New York in his car in record time. He stayed at an inn not far away and came over to our cottage in a powerful inboard launch with a sleek mahogany veneer. Sometimes he'd take us across the lake on wild rides, during which we'd cling to our seats as sheets of spray rose on either side.

My grandmother, a kind and unpretentious person, found the gatherings with her haughtier relatives stressful. She and Aunt

Margaret became panicky whenever these esteemed family members were due to visit. As they rushed around straightening things and working themselves into a lather, they reminded me and my siblings to be especially polite to our important guests. One summer, Aunt Jean visited us at the same time Aunt Dolly was in residence. The two of them fell into an argument about the Korean War, which was then raging. Dolly thought the U.S. should drop the atomic bomb on China if that was the only way to stop the Red Tide. Aunt Jean was outraged. She affected her sternest demeanour and told her sister that the Chinese came from a far more ancient and noble civilization than the Americans and that using the bomb against China was unthinkable. My grandmother weakly suggested that we all go out to the verandah for tea.

A bonus for me at Lake Rosseau was the chance for long, relaxed visits with my father. While he almost never got into the water and could hardly swim, he loved to lie out on the dock in a deck chair with his shirt open. He would snooze in the blazing sun until his face, his stomach and the fronts of his legs were lobster red. The rest of him remained his usual shade of pale white. While he suffered afterward from the sunburn, the rest of us laughed about the sharp lines on his body demarcating the zones of sun and no-sun. Once my father had settled in at the lake, having slept for most of several days, one of his favourite activities was to sing with us. He would run through the medley of British imperial ditties he had learned at school and then sing labour and socialist songs with gusto. These concerts, in which we participated lustily, were reserved for my mother, my siblings and me. He did not inflict the singing on my mother's family.

In the evenings, the five of us would often go for a rowboat ride close to the shore, where the great bluff soared above us. Gord and I took turns rowing. When my father heard frogs croaking in the twilight, he would imitate them loudly, hoping, he told us, to convince some lovesick frog that he was a potential mate. On one visit to the lake, my father decided to compose a lengthy poem about my mother. Everywhere we went — out in the rowboat, off for walks, outside eating sandwiches — he read aloud from the latest draft. This prompted much hilarity, especially when he reached the line that spoke of my mother's "limpid eyes."

One cloudless night, I stood outside with my father, staring up into the sky. Cold blue stars, strewn in all directions, glowed like sequins, making patterns little and big. When I looked down, the patterns were there below me as well, reflected in the still perfection of the lake. As I tilted again to take in the great swath of the Milky Way, my head swam.

These stars had been out there forever, my father told me. His voice was confident, full of fervour, as if he were revealing a great truth. After a minute, he corrected himself. Individual stars didn't last forever, he said, but as old ones burned out, new ones were born. Stars had always existed, and they always would. And it wasn't just that stars had been there forever, but that the universe extended infinitely in all directions. There was no end to it, no beginning. My brain went funny as I tried to think about that. No God had created this infinite realm, my father proclaimed.

As an adult, I would realize that my father was conveying the steady-state theory of the universe, a theory popular up until the middle of the twentieth century. Since then, it has been abandoned by most astronomers and physicists in favour of the big-bang theory, which holds that the universe was born at a finite point in the past, the product of an unimaginably stupendous explosion from an unimaginably tiny speck. This vision of a finite universe, which was born and which will die, is vastly different from my father's conception.

From the fate of the stars, he went on to give me an explanation for the origin of the Earth that is also out of favour today. A star, he told me, in a close encounter with the sun, had torn off a piece of material that swept out into space and gradually congealed into the nine planets of the solar system. On Earth, he told me, life evolved as a matter of chance, over an immensely long period of time. For him, the high point of evolution was the human species. It wasn't until years later that I understood how his theories of the universe and of evolution were intimately connected to his conviction that the highest form of life was moving inexorably toward Communism.

Nine

THE PARTY LINE

THE YEAR I TURNED ELEVEN, my father set up a study group for the children of local Communists. Seven or eight boys, including Gord and me — there were no girls in the group, as it happened — met on Saturday mornings in our living room. I knew the other kids well. They all lived close by, so they walked to our house or rode their bikes over. My mother was there to greet them, but she occupied herself with housework or went out and visited friends during our study sessions.

The group was presented to us as a way to have fun with our friends and learn at the same time. After we had assembled in the living room and made plans to play street hockey or ride our bikes after the session, my father would come in carrying a collection of books and articles. As he sat down in his favourite armchair, a rather lumpy affair with a flowered cover that had been faded by the sun, we took our places on the floor and faced him. I found the prospect of my father lecturing my friends a little embarrassing at first, but he quickly managed to subdue the group and get everyone's attention. The idea that he was going to initiate us into the beliefs of our parents, dealing with the subjects that they talked about at their meetings, was appealing enough to make us listen, and there was no horseplay at these gatherings. On bright days, the sun streamed through the living room window, casting my father in silhouette. As he proceeded through his material, his tone ranged from one of gentle persuasion to hectoring to angry and back again.

Over the five or six mornings we met, the story he told us — the scripture he was preaching — was that of Lenin and the Bolshevik Revolution. Lenin's brother, we learned, had participated in a failed attempt to assassinate the Russian czar, and he was captured and hanged. A sense of horror crept over me as I pictured him suspended with a rope around his neck. I knew we were supposed to be having fun during these sessions, but it was all so dismal. People were always being executed in these stories. It made me feel important that my father spent so much time with the group, but I couldn't wait for the lessons to be over so I could have lunch with the other kids and go outside.

My father explained to our Saturday morning group that the attempt by Lenin's brother to assassinate the czar had been a political error. It was always an error to engage in assassination politics, he said. It was wrong to substitute yourself for the masses, and it was incorrect to believe that the revolution could be made by anyone except the working class. That was why the romantic Narodniks in Russia, whose goal had been to organize a peasant uprising against the czarist regime, had been wrong.

The working class had to make the revolution, my father explained, despite the fact that it constituted only a small minority of the population of Russia, which was an overwhelmingly rural and agricultural country. The people committed to this approach were the Marxist social democrats. But they too had split along the way. At a conference of the Russian social democrats held in London, to keep them out of the grasp of the czar's police, the party had divided into two streams. The stream in the majority on a particular procedural vote, led by Lenin, claimed for itself the title Bolsheviks. "Bolshevik" meant "majority" in Russian. Those in the minority were called Mensheviks, the Russian word for "minority."

There was bad blood from then on between the Bolsheviks and the Mensheviks, my father said. As he saw it, the Mensheviks were too soft, too reformist. Only Lenin and the Bolsheviks combined a comprehension of capitalism with revolutionary toughness. When he told us that Lenin had very few followers for a considerable period of time, I asked how he could have continued to claim the title "Bolshevik." But my father shrugged off my question with good humour, commenting that my point was a mere formality.

What had seemed clear-cut at the beginning of our educational exercise became murky as the weeks went by. Only the working class could make the revolution, but revolution required a vanguard to act as a sort of midwife on the workers' behalf. In addition, almost every group working for large-scale change in Russia in the last years of the czarist regime — the Mensheviks, the Trotskyites, the Jewish Bund, the Social Revolutionaries — was in the wrong for some reason or another; all of these groups merited denunciation by my father. During those perilous times, only Lenin and his band of followers were the carriers of the true flame.

I was too young to question my father's world view in any serious way. Moreover, going along with him seemed to invite me, and the other kids, into a select, highly privileged group made up of the keepers of a precious truth. This was heady stuff. Still, it made me miserable to think about what he was saying. There was always so much killing, death and strife among those who were basically on the same side. I hated the way Communists denounced those who disagreed with them. Whenever my father read aloud from the works of the great leaders, the passage always involved trashing someone for being too soft and "parliamentarist" or too infantile and "adventurist." It was apparent to me, even then, that

Communists hated fellow leftists even more than they disliked the capitalist enemy.

What was monumentally perplexing to me was that personalities who were heroic in one historical situation became the objects of vitriol later on. Kamenev, Zinoviev and Bukharin were all heroes of the Bolshevik Revolution in 1917. No praise was too high for them then. But following show trials in Moscow in the 1930s, all three ended up in front of firing squads, as dangerous enemies of the revolution. My father's explanation for this sad state of affairs was that many people who had once been unflaggingly true to the cause had softened and gone corrupt.

Leon Trotksy was the ultimate example. Trotsky, my father taught us, was the great hero of the revolution of 1905, the leading orator in stirring up the masses in St. Petersburg. By 1917, though he was heroic as commander of the newly founded Red Army, Trotsky was already insisting on adhering to his own political line, one not exactly in accord with Lenin's. This was wrong, said my father. But I was confused. Hadn't Lenin received high praise for remaining so toughly independent of other social democrats, even when he was in the minority? Nonetheless, it was the Trotsky of the late 1920s and early 1930s who evoked the greatest amount of spittle from my father during our discussions. This Trotsky, with his talk of permanent revolution, in opposition to Stalin's theory of socialism in one country, was a villain of satanic proportions. Thankfully, my father spared us the story of Trotsky's murder in Mexico by an agent of Stalin's who was carrying a false Canadian passport. I suppose he didn't want us to know that Stalin's hirelings went around stabbing people in the head with ice picks.

While I was in no position at eleven to dispute the idea of a vanguard party, I did have the sinking feeling that deciding which group constituted the real vanguard was no easy thing. It all seemed to come down to a no-holds-barred fight among the leaders to determine who was the real successor to Marx and who were the "false prophets."

Integral to the concept of the vanguard, we learned over our weeks of lectures, was the Communist idea of democracy. Communists subscribed to something called "democratic centralism." The way this worked was that, at various times, there was open debate among members about doctrine, strategy and tactics. Once the key organs of the party had resolved these questions, however, the decisions were to be accepted without further debate. Iron adherence was expected. The interpretation of the party line on a day-to-day basis remained in the hands of the top decision-making bodies, and particularly in the hands of the General Secretary of the Communist Party of the Soviet Union, whose awesome legitimacy flowed directly from the fact that he could trace his lineage back to Marx. But how did you know when you were allowed to debate a particular question? I wondered silently. Did the top leaders decide that too?

The next thing we learned in our Saturday morning sessions was that membership in the vanguard was open only to a select few. You had to undergo a period of probation before becoming a full-fledged member of the Party. And you had to pass tests in Marxist theory before you were admitted. Party members disdained mass-membership organizations like the British Labour Party, where people simply signed a card and paid a small fee to join. The vanguard party had to be fit and tough, an instrument for concerted political action. Any other point of view was roundly denounced as evidence of bourgeois morality. Indeed, Communists prided themselves on their independence from sentimentalism and bourgeois morality, insisting that there were no absolute moral standards — that all morality in the end was class morality, deriving its validity from its utility in advancing the victory of the working class.

Once he had taught us about the theory and practice of the vanguard party, my father returned to the point of the exercise: the revolutionary transformation of society, which lay not too far off. Whenever I asked him how long it would be until the socialist revolution, he always gave me the same answer — about ten years. The revolution, he told our little group, would begin a new chapter in human history. The human race was still in its infancy, and it was about to take a huge step forward. What would emerge from the revolution would be no less than a "new man," my father explained. That was the point of it all, the justification for the enormous effort, the risks, the conflict and the persecution.

The idea of the new man captivated my father. It was the centre of his passion, his Communism. His faith was rooted there rather than in the strivings of actual living people for a better life. He believed he had a role to play in the greatest act of creation in human history, and he dreamed of this new day. As for me, I didn't find the prospect of the new man comforting. It felt cold, almost monstrous. Whenever my father mentioned him, I pictured a giant. In my mind, the new man was much like the statues and posters I had seen in photos and films about the Soviet Union, where idealized working men and women were depicted in heroic, oversized guises. The thought that we were bringing to life a being so much more powerful and advanced than ourselves left me uneasy. But how could I be against it? It was the ultimate goal of everything my parents stood for.

I much preferred what my father had taught me about the stars when we were up at the lake. Who knew what went on out there, in those beckoning worlds? At the very least, it couldn't be worse than what was happening in this one.

Ten

AT CAMP WITHOUT A PADDLE

FAR FROM THE ANXIETY CREATED by the idea of the new man, there was a left-wing Jewish nirvana, where we kids spent weeks in the summer — Camp Naivelt. It was the wackiest place I have yet encountered. Nestled in a circle of hills just west of Brampton, Ontario, this was a camp unlike any other.

In the early fifties, Camp Naivelt — Naivelt means "new world" in Yiddish — was a mecca for Toronto's large left-wing Jewish community. The camp was associated with the United Jewish People's Order (UJPO), which in turn had close ties with the Communist LPP. During the winter, I hung out a lot at the UJPO's large cultural centre, which was not far from our house. My father was often involved in meetings there.

The ample facilities of the UJPO served all age groups. In the dining area at one end sat throngs of elderly men — many of whom had been garment workers — eating their lunch, speaking Yiddish and playing cribbage. This is where old friends got together, especially on Sundays. Dance and crafts classes were held in other parts of the building. Films were often shown in the evenings.

Before Torontonians voted to legalize Sunday sports in 1954, the city was like a graveyard on Sundays. I hated the greyness. I would stand outside our house watching bits of newspaper blowing down the street. No cars were moving. Nothing was happening. So on Sunday mornings, Gord and I went to the UJPO to play floor hockey with the kids of other leftie parents. While most of the kids were Jewish, a sizable number were not.

In the UJPO's large auditorium, dramas, musicals, concerts and children's plays were constantly on offer. The major cultural icons of the North American Left were regularly on display; Paul Robeson and Pete Seeger performed, along with the Travellers, a well-known Canadian folk-singing group. Many of the songs they sang would become famous a decade later in the great folk revival of the sixties.

During our years in Ottawa, Paul Robeson had once dined at our little house on Flora Street while on a concert tour. I couldn't remember anything of that visit, but I was enthralled by his performances at the UJPO and Camp Naivelt. I marvelled at the power of his voice, although I was more caught up in its sheer velocity than in its artistry. At one concert, I noticed that Robeson held his hand in front of one of his ears as he hit and held those huge notes. I was told he had to do this to prevent his voice from damaging his hearing. Imagine that, I thought, someone with a voice so strong he could hurt himself.

If I was too young to comprehend the greatness of Robeson's singing, I knew the outlines of his amazing life. He was an all-American college football star who had gone on to huge success as a singer. By the end of the 1920s, he had also become the most highly praised black actor in the United States. But his membership in the Communist Party embroiled him in constant battles with the U.S. government. For a time, the U.S. government withdrew Robeson's passport, thus preventing him from leaving the country to perform abroad. During that period, Robeson did two concerts from the back of a flatbed truck on the American side of the border at Peace Arch Park, south of Vancouver, for audiences in both countries.

Camp Naivelt was the UJPO's idea of civilization writ large. It was a huge piece of rolling farmland dotted with hundreds of cabins that people could lease for their families on a long-term basis. Unlike the cottages that would be bought by the next generation of Jewish Torontonians, the camp was communal. It had the feel of a kibbutz.

The cabins were rectangular wooden buildings, with one or two rudimentary bedrooms, a bathroom and a kitchen–living room area. They were located on three hills that surrounded the central valley, through which the Credit River flowed. Hills One, Two and Three each had their own mini-administrations. They had their own identities, too, and a considerable amount of rivalry existed. Hill One was distant from the others and somewhat standoffish. Hill Three was newer and more rudimentary, which left Hill Two as the most civilized of the three. For a time, I felt sure Hill Two was the golden mean for the planet.

In the valley beside the river were the camp's amenities, which were far from posh. There was a huge, one-storey wooden dining hall with a vast kitchen. Hundreds of people could be served at a sitting on the long wooden tables. A few hundred yards away was the camp's pride and joy — the swimming pool. An auditorium for concerts and films stood on an island in the middle of the river that was connected to the mainland by a bridge.

On Sunday afternoons in summer, Camp Naivelt was a bustling town. Thousands of people milled up and down between the dining hall and the swimming pool. Many of them were staying in the cabins, but hordes of others had driven out for the day. On such afternoons, my brother and I and our toddler sister joined the procession, walking back and forth under the relentless sun with my mother and father. Not until years later, when I saw thousands of people out for promenades in French and Italian towns, did I witness anything quite like it. At Camp Naivelt, though, those out for a stroll were not on a promenade beside the Mediterranean with pastel villas in the background. They were walking alongside a small, not particularly beautiful river and across a flat field, whose grass was completely beaten down, next to a dusty road.

The quintessential Camp Naivelt man was attired in dark, loose-fitting shorts that extended to just above the knee. Shirts, which varied from the button-up variety to undershirts, were always tucked in. Black dress shoes and dark socks completed the outfit. The typical man was short and balding, with a stooped posture, a large pot-shaped belly, thin arms and spindly hairless legs. As they strolled very slowly in large groups, many of these men puffed on cigars. Cigar smoke perfumed the still, hot air. When borscht and rye bread were served in the dining hall, the cigars came inside also. Maybe they helped drive away some of the omnipresent flies. People spent much of their time swishing flies off their bread, hoping the insects would land on the dozens of strips of sticky flypaper hanging down from the ceilings. There were plenty of carcasses on the flypaper, but it never seemed to cut down the fly population in the hall.

My father was a big wheel at Camp Naivelt. Wherever he walked, pot-bellied men came up to greet him. In the dining hall, he sat surrounded by bald heads, which nodded sagely as he spoke. Sometimes he ran political educationals for forty or fifty Party members in the dining room between meals, in the mornings and afternoons. I would sometimes stand outside and listen to his voice, which was full of conviction as he emphasized some particular point.

The kids' camp at Camp Naivelt, also known rather hilariously as the Colony, was nestled just below Hills Two and Three. It ran from the beginning of July to late August. Because my father was an LPP organizer, we got a special deal. Camp for my siblings and me was twenty-five dollars a week each.

The Colony was equipped with a dozen bunkhouses strung in a line atop a field that sloped upward from the river. Behind these were the woods and a massive toilet facility and washing area, known as the Ritz. The bunkhouses, known as "bunks," were plain wooden buildings with open rafters. Each had room for about fifteen kids and one counsellor. The camp had bunks for boys and bunks for girls and was for kids aged six to thirteen. At age thirteen, you became a counsellor in training, or CIT, and after that a full-fledged counsellor.

At other summer camps, kids learned how to paddle a canoe. They went on canoe trips and camped out in the woods. They mastered the art of horseback-riding, perfected their ability to do the Australian crawl, practised their dives until they became expert. Perhaps they learned archery or immersed themselves in arts and crafts. They whittled bits of wood, discovered the joys of papier mâché and learned about the beasts and flora of the forests.

Things were different at Camp Naivelt. A day there began with the sounding of a loud horn. This directed the bleary-eyed campers to rise, dress and proceed to the Ritz. They were then to hasten to the centre of the field, where there was a small wooden statue of an aeroplane and a flagpole. The statue was dedicated to a Jewish Canadian airman who had flown twenty-four missions over Nazi Germany before being shot down and killed.

When enough of the campers had assembled, the camp director, an impossibly thin, very tall man dressed from head to toe in white (including a white gob hat, circular with a little fringe), called for order by blowing the whistle that dangled from a string around his neck. We solemnly sang "O Canada!" I wondered if our director, whose name was Chuck, took off the whistle when he was taking a shower or when he retired to bed.

Chuck, believing his young charges should rise and retire early, had put the Colony on standard time, although everyone else in the province, including the rest of Camp Naivelt, was on daylight savings time. The popular radio station of the day was CHUM 1050, which gave the time as "CHUM time, two o'clock." In the Colony, we referred to CHUCK time. Endless confusion was created by the time change. It was chaos every Sunday morning when parents drove out from the city to see their kids. This was unfortunate, since these visits were already emotional enough. When parents arrived, their kids were upbeat, carefree, having a wonderful experience. By the time they were about to leave, many kids were sobbing uncontrollably. Some of them had to be helped back to their bunks while Mom and Dad made their getaway.

Another of Chuck's ideas was that democracy should be taught to his charges at an early age. He announced that each bunkhouse was to elect a representative to a campers' council. My bunk elected me, and the first meeting of the council was held in the small director's HQ, with Chuck serving as chairman.

The compulsory morning singing of "O Canada!" was on my mind. The kids in my bunk thought it would be better to sleep in a little longer, skip the national anthem and head straight to the dining hall for breakfast. I raised the issue at the meeting, arguing that the song should be optional. Sensing support from other members of the council, I moved a formal resolution to that effect. Chuck spoke against the resolution and called the question. All but two members of the council voted for my motion. Chuck then announced that he would not go along with the vote and declared that campers had to show up for the ceremony whether they liked it or not. The council never met again. We were certainly learning about democracy.

I wasn't all that surprised at Chuck's response to my attempted coup. I had already seen him in action during a Communist election campaign in Toronto. He and I were assigned to go around one Saturday afternoon to try to convince local shopkeepers to put up LPP posters in their windows. Outside a barbershop, Chuck tried to persuade me to go inside and ask the barber. I objected that I had never done this kind of thing before. He assured me it would be easy. I stuck to my guns and insisted that he teach me how. Chuck went inside and showed the barber the election poster. The barber told him to get the hell out of his shop. That ended our efforts for the day.

Possibly those who ran the Colony thought it would be a good idea to include some political education in our life there. In practice, though, they never did anything about it. There was the odd attempt to tell children Jewish folk tales, but such events usually fell flat. The camp's anarchism overcame any efforts to direct the thinking of the kids or the adults who spent their summers there. Whether by design or by happy accident, there were no thought police at Camp Naivelt.

The closest thing to propaganda were the concerts performed for packed houses in the auditorium on the little island in the Credit River. On hot summer evenings the kids from the Colony would squeeze into seats among the adult campers from the three hills. I can still picture Pete Seeger carrying his stool and his banjo out onto the bare stage. He would talk and sing and tell stories of the political struggles of working people from many countries. In South Africa, he told us, the government would not let people hold meetings of protest. So they had to make use of songs with no overt political message. One of them was "Everybody Loves Saturday Night." The authorities could hardly object to that innocuous message. Thousands would gather to sing it, repeating the main line again and again, with rising passion, and then they would sing it in French: "Tout le monde aime samedi soir." And then in other languages. As he spoke, Seeger began to sing, first softly and then with ever-greater force, keeping time on the floor with his large right foot. Before long, we were all singing, until the auditorium was alive with energy. We were a vessel bound for a better world.

The food at Camp Naivelt was soggy and tasteless, with ingredients you could not identify if you closed your eyes. As phlegmatic personnel brought out large platters of food from the kitchen, booing from the campers was not uncommon. After meals, on the way back to our bunks, we often saw Hymie, the short, bald man who was in charge of purchasing supplies for the kitchen. We made up a ditty sung to the tune of "We Shall Not Be Moved": "Hymie is our leader, he shall be removed." If Hymie ever heard the song, he showed no sign of it.

Supplementing our diet with snacks purchased at the camp's little shop became a major preoccupation. Each kid was supposed to have two dollars a week to spend on these goodies, but that was not enough. Gambling was one way to raise extra cash. During "rest period" after lunch, many campers learned how to play variations of poker and blackjack.

My friend Steve and I hit on a highly unusual way to raise money. One day we saw Director Chuck hurrying across the field, looking more than usually agitated. He asked us to accompany him to a water pump near the Ritz. Chuck got down on his knees and examined the pump. He asked us to lift the pump up so he could put some water purifier into the well. Chuck opened the box and poured in some of its contents. Then, seeming puzzled, he reread the instructions on the box and emptied more purifier into the well. When the exercise was complete, Steve and I decided not to drink any water for the next few days. Instead, we used our funds to buy grape soda, our beverage of choice at the time.

A few days later, a major outbreak of diarrhoea struck the Colony. Dozens of campers stampeded for the Ritz. The lineups for the few available toilets were lengthy and, for those in need, they moved agonizingly slowly. Steve and I, who were not afflicted, joined the line. When we got close to the toilets, we sold our places to people in dire straits.

Even if we didn't have the usual camp amenities at the Colony, we did have the swimming pool, and each bunk swam there once a day. One summer, though, there was a continual shortage of water that closed the pool for days at a time. The water shortage was partly explained by the hot, dry weather, but it was mainly the result of an experiment that went wrong.

For some reason, the powers that be at Camp Naivelt had decided that they wanted more water to flow through the eastern arm of the Credit River, which circled the island, than through the western arm, which fed the swimming pool. Volunteers equipped with shovels and spades had gone up to the camp that spring expressly to dig out a wider, deeper entrance to the eastern arm. I witnessed some of their heroic work, which I thought had been inspired by the great dams and hydroelectric projects that were the pride of Stalin's Soviet Union.

The diversion had worked too well, however, leaving the western arm of the river a shallow trickle. That summer the campers in the Colony had a new activity. Each day we were herded, with much grumbling, down to the river. Our orders were to dig out the western arm of the river. We had only a few shovels; most of us were expected to pick up rocks and handfuls of clay and earth and throw them onto the shore. Few of us had any real aptitude for the work. But the digging did take the place of swimming, the one real activity we ever actually had at the camp.

The Colony was not the only camp with links to the LPP that sent its campers out to work. Each summer we were bussed from Camp Naivelt to a sister Ukrainian camp near Palermo, Ontario. Trips to Palermo helped quiet any sentiment that we were hard done by at the Colony. The camp there was on a piece of land so flat it could have been in Manitoba. There were few trees, and the cabins looked as if they might actually be in the Ukraine. In the centre of this flat terrain, there was a statue of a Ukrainian poet. Swimming was in the muddy local river, which was reached by climbing down crumbling cliffs. I went swimming there once with my mother, on the occasion of some sort of celebration at the camp. It was a very hot day, and we were anxious to get away from the endless speeches. Once in the water, though, I went out a little too far and got caught in the current. I lost control. My head went under, and all I could see was the yellow-black water. A hand reached down and pulled me up. It was my mother.

The masters of the camp at Palermo seemed to think they were running a collective farm, and the kids there were required to help raise their own vegetables. We saw the little vegetable patches behind their cabins. After a day at Palermo, the dining hall and Hymie didn't look so bad.

The main activity at the Colony was hanging out. Once you became a CIT, you were expected to spend some of your time supervising other campers. For one whole summer, I spent most of my time supervising my friend Steve, who was two years younger. We bought bottles of grape soda and headed down to the river. Sometimes we walked a mile or two along the banks, well outside the camp, to an area where there were high earthen cliffs. Here we found ant colonies and once witnessed a war between red ants and black ones.

On rare occasions, Chuck would organize an outing. One summer he decided that the dozen or so older kids should go to Stratford, about fifty miles away, to see a performance of *Henry V* and attend a jazz evening with Duke Ellington. It was a great idea; only in their execution did Chuck's ideas develop flaws. He scrounged a large truck and had a friend deliver us to a farmer's field outside Stratford the night before. We bedded down in the barn, sleeping in the bedrolls we had brought with us. The next day, dirty and wrecked from our night in the hay, we walked into town. But the concert was fantastic. The musicians' rendition of "When the Saints Go Marching In" built up and up until the rafters rang and I thought I was in heaven.

With so much time on their hands, the campers in the Colony often got up to no good. The worst-behaved camper was Zalman Yanovsky, who later became famous as a member of the rock group the Lovin' Spoonful, although Steve's sister Joyce ran Zalman a close second. The evening meetings of counsellors and cits were largely devoted to discussions of their antics. One time Zalman hitchhiked back to Toronto, and anxious hours passed before his whereabouts were discovered. He founded a group called the Fartnabies, whose initiation rite involved drinking a small quantity of urine. Membership was restricted to boys, and one of their favourite activities was to run naked through a girls' bunk in the evening. They also enjoyed breaking into the camp director's office and recording their own bizarre announcements to replace those carefully prepared by Chuck.

At night, many campers turned their minds to evil deeds against each other and their counsellors. Short-sheeting beds was a favoured gambit. You remade the victim's bed after folding the bottom sheet in half; when he tried to climb inside, he could only make it halfway. Putting toads, frogs and garter snakes under the top sheet was also popular. One summer we had a counsellor who stayed out late with his girlfriend every night. Once the counsellors' flashlight patrol had gone through to check on us, we were up and out, often for hours, sneaking off through the woods to the hills. Some of us knew families on Hills Two and Three. If we were lucky, we could spend the night playing cards in one of the cabins. One night, upon our return, we removed our counsellor's mattress from his bed and hoisted it over the rafters.

If Camp Naivelt lacked canoes, it did have boys and girls in close proximity. As you advanced through the ranks to the status of CIT and then counsellor, romance became an ever more absorbing obsession. A mild whiff was evident during the instruction we received in artificial respiration. In those days, mouth-to-mouth resuscitation had not been conceived. Instead, the supposed victim would lie face down with hands under the face and elbows stretched out to the sides. The rescuer would kneel at the victim's head, press down on his or her back and then pull up the victim's arms from just above the elbows. Endless repetitions ensued. It did not take clever young males long to figure out that if the right female practised this procedure on you, it could be very agreeable. But romance also took more overt forms. When I was thirteen, a girl named Pat, who had short black hair and brown eyes, picked me out for her attention. Early one evening, I was standing between two bunks when Pat came walking up. Without a word, she kissed me on the mouth. On the teeth, actually, since I was just opening my mouth to say something. She applied herself to me for a few seconds, and then it was over. The next evening Pat was back again. This time she took me by the hand, and we walked silently down the long slope to the area beside the swimming pool, where we were surrounded by other couples. With more practice, I finally got the hang of kissing.

While I was at Camp Naivelt, it was the only place on earth. At the beginning of the summer, when the days were endlessly long, I thought of nothing but the adventures to come in the Colony, the little world nestled among Hills One, Two and Three. But soon enough the days grew shorter, and harsher realities would have to be faced.

Eleven

UNCLE JOE

IT WAS SOMETIME IN 1952 that I first heard the names Julius and Ethel Rosenberg. The Rosenbergs, a married couple who lived in New York City, had been charged with espionage against the United States. In proceedings that began in the summer of 1950, it was alleged that Julius Rosenberg had asked his brother-in-law David Greenglass, who had worked on the Manhattan Project, to obtain information for the Soviets on the components needed to build the atomic bomb. At the end of their sensational trial, the Rosenbergs were found guilty. Judge Irving Kaufman sentenced both husband and wife to die in the electric chair.

I became aware of the plight of the Rosenbergs only after they had been sentenced. A worldwide campaign was mounted to save them. Albert Einstein, Pablo Picasso and Jean-Paul Sartre were among those who petitioned for clemency. For Canadian Communists and a large number of their liberalminded fellow citizens, the campaign to stop the execution became a *cause célèbre*. Demonstrations were mounted, petitions were presented for people to sign on the streets, and many public meetings were held.

My own anguished recognition of the impending execution came after reading a flyer distributed by local Communists. One panel featured a drawing of a man and a woman sitting side by side in electric chairs, holding hands. I couldn't stop thinking about that image. How long did it take to die in the electric chair? Would you feel any pain, or would you become unconscious as soon as they turned the power on? What would it be like to sit in a jail cell counting down the days until you were to be electrocuted? Would they use the same chair to execute both of the Rosenbergs? Which one of them would die first?

As the campaign to save the Rosenbergs dragged on, I feared that their case could be a warning for the members of my own family. Julius and Ethel Rosenberg had children too, I knew. That summer we were visiting the Lake Rosseau cottage rented by my grandparents. One rainy morning, I ran into the boathouse where we were staying and found my parents sitting side by side with their backs to the window. It was obvious that I had burst in on an important conversation. My father leaned forward on his elbows, but it was my mother who spoke first: "Jimmy, we have something we want to talk to you about." I felt apprehensive. She often used those words when she had bad news.

"You know about the Rosenbergs," my father said softly. I said yes. For an instant, I thought he was going to say that they had been put to death. I was relieved to hear that the execution had not yet taken place, but what he told me next renewed my sense of dread. The Rosenbergs were not spies, he explained; they were being persecuted, and would likely die, for their political views. "This is a warning for all Communists," he said.

Perhaps in response to my obvious terror, my father continued on to say reassuringly that such a thing was less likely to happen in Canada than in the U.S. But if he and my mother were ever arrested, he told me, we had plenty of relatives and friends who would look after my siblings and me. In that instant, the full horror of everything we had been living through, the misery of being in a little group hated by everyone else, came home to me. Now my family could be the target. *I* could be the target.

My parents and their comrades talked about McCarthyism all the time. I didn't really understand who McCarthy was. All I knew was that some terrible force had taken shape in the United States and that it placed Communists in deep peril. Even on the Canadian side of the border, the storm was apparently gathering strength, and we were a tiny group up against the maelstrom. I had vague fears that my father's connections to the Soviet Union could get us into trouble. From time to time, he made reference to the way the Soviets helped finance the Party in Canada through retail outlets where Soviet goods were sold.

Well before Joseph McCarthy, the Republican junior senator from Wisconsin, launched his campaign against supposed Communists holding government posts, the Red Scare was underway in the United States. In 1947, the House Un-American Activities Committee (HUAC) began its investigation of the motion picture industry in Hollywood. Making use of "friendly" witnesses, they zeroed in on a group of people accused of holding left-wing views. Ten of those named, to become famous as the Hollywood Ten, refused to answer any of HUAC's questions, citing their constitutional rights. The ten were found guilty of contempt of Congress, and each of them was sentenced to between six and twelve months in prison.

One of the ten, Edward Dmytryk, appeared before HUAC in April 1951 and named twenty-six former members of left-wing groups. Those names were added to the growing blacklist. As the process continued, the Hollywood studios barred hundreds of people from working, including Charlie Chaplin, Dashiell Hammett, Lillian Hellman, Burl Ives, Pete Seeger, Orson Welles and Paul Robeson.

There were also direct efforts to shut down the U.S. Communist Party. Party leaders were arrested and charged with violating the Alien Registration Act, passed in June 1940, which made it illegal for anyone in the U.S. to advocate or otherwise support the over-throw of the United States government. In October 1949, eleven Party members were convicted. Over the following two years, forty-six others were accused of advocating the overthrow of the government.

In February 1950, Joseph McCarthy announced to a women's club in Wheeling, West Virginia, "I have here in my hand a list of 205 [State Department employees] who have been named as members of the Communist Party...and who nevertheless are still work-ing and shaping the policy of the State Department." McCarthy's speech struck a chord among Americans fearful of internal sub-version. The senator, who became famed for his abusive language and his unwarranted tarring of people's reputations, began receiv-ing fresh information from J. Edgar Hoover, the head of the FBI. McCarthy became chairman of the U.S. Senate's Government Operations Committee and its permanent investigations subcom-mittee, which allowed him to investigate government departments. He called many witnesses before the committee, brutally accusing them of being subversives and informing them bluntly that the only way to clear their names was to name other left-wingers. For the next five years, his witch hunt gave rise to fear and hysteria across the U.S.

There were powerful echoes of McCarthy's anti-red crusade on the Canadian side of the border. Conservative and Social Credit MPs repeatedly called on the Liberal government to resur-rect Section 98 of the Criminal Code, which had been repealed before the war. Section 98 would have allowed Communists to be criminally prosecuted for sedition, and it could have been used to prosecute and imprison the top leaders of the Party. The anti-Communist fury of the time was promoted not only by politicians and newspaper editorials but by professional associations and pri-vate sector companies that hunted for Communists in their ranks.

Canadair, the jet aircraft manufacturer, published a newspaper ad stating, "Everywhere are evidences of the continuous underground, cancerous movements of Communism and its infiltration into our way of life."

The Soviet Union and its leader were objects of scorn in the newspapers every day. The front page of the paper I delivered was full of stories about Stalin and "red spies." When I asked my father why there were so many stories in the paper about executions, trials of officials and labour camps in the Soviet Union, he sat me down and explained patiently that the newspapers were printing deliberate lies. His answer didn't surprise me, since I was used to the idea that Communists were persecuted. But it did puzzle me. I wondered how he could distinguish the lies from the truth in the newspapers. In my literal-minded way, I thought there might be some simple way to tell what was true and what was a lie. It occurred to me that perhaps the lies were printed in italics.

I was also bothered by the fact that the Communist Party was the only political party in the Soviet Union. Why were there no others? I asked my father. People were happy with the building of socialism there, he replied; they simply did not want to have other political parties. This answer ate away at me. In Canada, if you didn't like the party in power, you could vote for another one. My parents always did. It was second nature to me to think that criticizing the government was the essence of democracy. So I probed further. "You mean not one single person in the whole country would like to have another party?" I asked my father.

That question elicited a more elaborate answer. Under capitalism, he clarified, no matter which party governed, the capitalist class was always in power. This was the dictatorship of the capitalist class. Even though there were a number of political parties, the capitalists were so powerful that they could always force the government to do their bidding. After the socialist revolution, he continued, but before socialism had actually been fully established, there would have to be a period in which the proletariat ran its own dictatorship.

My father could tell from the look on my face that I wasn't taking this idea too well. He explained patiently that a dictatorship of the proletariat would be much more democratic, because the proletariat was the majority of the population. Once this phase was over and socialism had been fully established, the dictatorship would end. No one would want to go back to capitalism, and everyone could look forward to the full achievement of Communism. With Communism, he said, money would disappear. Everyone would get what they needed, and everyone would work for the common good. The state would disappear, and it would not matter much who headed the government. Anyone could do the job because it would be so unimportant.

At times, in my agony, I wondered if our family would be better off moving to Russia. There, at least, the politics of my parents wouldn't be a problem. When I mentioned this idea to my father, he told me that our struggle was here in Canada, not in Russia. Besides, he said, he preferred to live here. I knew I didn't actually want to go to Russia anyway. Why, then, couldn't we just live like everybody else? My parents could have their ideas, I thought, but why couldn't they be quieter about them? We knew other Communists who led normal lives, with the father working at a regular job. Those people went to meetings at night, but nobody knew about their political affiliations. When they walked down the street, their neighbours were not always thinking that they were aliens.

I began to try even harder than usual to keep my own life on Melita Street in a watertight compartment. But with the McCarthyite mood of the times, that was impossible. The two worlds collided when my mother answered the phone one day and was asked by the woman at the other end whether we rented to "coloured people." My mother answered yes, and a few hours later, a woman named Jean Daniels and her niece, Minerva, arrived at the house. Jean, a Communist supporter, was from Halifax, Nova Scotia, where there had been a large black community for decades. She had got my parents' phone number through the political grapevine.

A few days later, Jean and Minerva moved into the third floor of our house. Their arrival caused a stir on Melita Street, whose population was one hundred per cent white at the time. Not everyone was pleased to have black people as neighbours, and a man who lived several doors down announced that he was going to draft a petition to let Jean and Minerva know they were not welcome. One evening eight or nine neighbours arrived at our door and asked to speak to my father. He invited them cordially into the living room. He listened to what they had to say, and then told them he would rent to whomever he liked. With that, the neighbours trooped out. The petition idea brewed for a while, but eventually its would-be originator dropped it. I was confused about blacks myself, having grown up in a world in which the only distinction that mattered was between Jews and non-Jews. My sister Linda thought Jean and Minerva were Jewish at first, and the thought also flashed through my mind.

Both women soon became close family friends. For me, Jean was like a second mother. She was a round woman with a huge laugh, magnetic and affectionate. She was also an avid hockey fan who listened to games on the radio with me. Once when she lived in Halifax, she told me, she went to a junior hockey game, where she grew so engrossed that every time her team scored she pounded the stranger in the seat in front on his shoulders. And we soon discovered that Jean couldn't hold a tune. No matter what she sang, it came out flat. We would get her to join in a song with us and then suddenly stop singing. Jean would sing a line or two more, until she realized what we were doing. Then we would all laugh until the tears came.

Twelve

DREAMS AND POLITICS

ONE MORNING IN JANUARY 1954, I was playing a hockey card game I had invented when my mother came into the room. "Grandpa died this morning," she said with icy calm. The news did not seem heavy, which surprised me. No one really close to me had ever died, and I thought you were supposed to feel shocked. I had had lunch three days earlier with my grandfather. On that occasion, when someone asked him how it felt to be eighty-one, he had answered, "Not so good." My mother's initially unruffled response to her father's death guided me, but that afternoon, when I walked past her bedroom, I heard her crying. Two days later, my grandfather's open coffin lay in the living room at my grandparents' house in North Toronto. My grandfather looked peaceful and quite natural. I did not attend his funeral, since my parents thought I was too young to be there. It took me a long time to figure out that a great light had gone out of my life.

THE MIDDLE-CLASS DREAM of the 1950s was slow to arrive in our household. We didn't have a television set until a couple of years later than most of our neighbours. And we had no car. These were the two acquisitions that mattered most to people on our street, although there were others as well. Refrigerators were fast replacing ice boxes, and oil furnaces were supplanting coal. When we first moved to our house on Melita Street, the ice man delivered blocks of ice a couple of times a week, and my dad went down to the basement in his undershirt in winter to shovel coal into the furnace. Now all of that was changing.

Most of my friends had television sets. When I visited them in the afternoons, we watched Westerns. The tinny sound, the dark shadows and the way the gangs of men on horseback looked like giant ants on the little black-and-white screens—none of this could diminish the romance of watching moving pictures at home. I wanted a television so badly I would often dream that we had one. One happy day when my father was out of town, my mother took us on the bus down to an appliance store called George's, whose slogan was "Let George Do It." We found a TV housed in a big blond wooden cabinet. It looked beautiful in the store, and I could hardly breathe thinking about the joys it would bring us. My mother bought it on the instalment plan and George's delivered it. I spent hours fiddling with the rabbit ears, trying to coax as many signals as possible out of the wonderful machine.

We got a car many months after the arrival of the television set, but it came to us in an unusual way. Jean and Minerva had moved out by then, and one day our upstairs tenant, a happy-go-lucky young guy who could seldom raise the money to pay his rent, simply moved and left behind his ancient convertible and a set of keys. We were terribly excited.

When my father turned the key in the ignition, the battery was dead. But it was not uncommon in those days to push cars down the street to get them going or to park them at the top of a hill to give them a rolling start. Since our street was flat, we rounded up other kids and pushed the car with my dad behind the wheel. It coughed and sputtered but wouldn't start. Finally a neighbour came out and pushed us with his own car. This time, the convertible roared to life, spewing thick blue smoke into the street. We leapt aboard and drove to my grandmother's house. Whenever we hit a red light, my mother put her foot on the accelerator while my father braked to keep the car from stalling.

Most of the clothes my siblings and I wore were second-hand, many of them obtained from my father's expanding and increasingly middle-class family in Montreal. Sometimes I hated these clothes. One winter coat had loops and wooden clasps up the front in place of regular buttons or a zipper. My mother told me it was the latest thing in Montreal, but I didn't care about that. On our street, being avant-garde where clothes were concerned was not a good thing. Whenever you got a haircut or went outside wearing a new pair of shoes, the other kids razzed you. "New shoes, new shoes," we would chant until the exasperated victim chased us down the street. A developmentally challenged boy named Teddy, who was about twenty years old, used to chase the kids who mocked him with the chant "Teddy shaves, Teddy shaves." New shoes or haircuts led to fistfights, not kudos, on Melita Street.

One spring day when I was twelve, I was walking up Christie Street and saw the girl of my dreams. She had the prettiest face, blue eyes and hair that was a little darker than blond. As she walked by with a couple of her friends, I felt the world going funny. Who was she, and where did she live? A few days later, I caught a glimpse of her walking down Ashworth, the street that ran parallel to Melita the next block over. Later still, I learned that her name was Irene and that she lived right across the back lane. With great excitement, I discovered that from the back room of our house I could see the kitchen in her house. In the evenings, I would sit in the dark looking out the window, hoping she would walk into the kitchen. When she did, I was intoxicated. The few times I saw her on the street, though, my nerve failed me. I managed to say hello, but that was about all.

One early autumn day in 1954, my brother Gord and I were out delivering our newspapers. The rain was beating down as I had never felt it before, and the violent wind was driving it into our faces. We were soaked to the skin by the time we'd put our papers into our carrier bags and flung them down on our wagon. At the bottom of one hill on our route, our wagon actually floated.

Everyone was talking about a hurricane named Hazel. The story was that the tail end of it would hit Toronto. When Gord and I had finished our route, we went home, stripped off all our clothes and put on new ones. We felt good. We had stood up to Hazel. We went downstairs to see a foot of water in the basement of our house.

When we went to bed that night, radio newscasts were saying that the worst was over. But as we slept, the Humber River in the city's west end was transformed into a raging torrent. The river burst its banks and overtook the houses on the plain beside it. More than eighty people died in the greatest natural disaster ever to strike the city.

The day after the hurricane was beautiful and crisp. I rode my bike for miles and miles, out to the river, where I saw the remains of a bridge that had been torn out by the wild torrent. Later I stood on the street, having just finished delivering my papers, looking at the fallen branches, and drinking a Coke. Despite the disaster, everything felt good to me.

Escape into teen fantasies and the fury of nature took me only so far, however. The year following the execution of the Rosenbergs, I started grade nine at Oakwood Collegiate. Oakwood was an unusual school, especially if you were the son of a full-time Communist organizer who by then had made it onto the Party's Central Committee. In a country that was not particularly militaristic — in the fifties, Canada was the only major country in the West without compulsory service in the armed forces for young men — Oakwood was a stronghold of fervent militarists. Most of the male teachers had served in the armed forces in the First or Second World War. In class, we were required to address them by their military rank.

My history teacher, Captain Henderson, was a lanky, loose-limbed man who treated his classes to bombastic attacks on Communists and Communism. He had made it his personal mission to warn his students about the danger of the Red Menace. Captain Henderson could be talking about anything when he would suddenly pull himself up to his full height and get off a line about the subversives who were undermining our country. I wasn't sure if he knew what my father did for a living, but I did know that I was being ground down by what I now labelled in my mind as McCarthyism. I watched the clock on the wall of the captain's classroom, counting down the minutes. Every jump of the hand brought me a little closer to getting out of there.

It was a bad time, and I felt things closing in on me. For years, I had mostly managed to keep my neighbourhood life separate from the politics of my parents, but that wasn't working any more. I began inventing a new world in my head to which I could escape. Whenever possible I stayed home from school, faking it at times, using the excuse that I had another sore throat. I became an expert at heating up oral thermometers on light bulbs and then shaking them down to the desired temperature, say 101 or 102. You didn't want the temperature to read 105, or your mother might call an ambulance.

I found my solace in books, even if I wasn't learning much about them from the Colonel Blimps at Oakwood. I identified with Jim, the hero of Robert Louis Stevenson's *Treasure Island*, and I was greatly consoled to learn that Stevenson had been a sickly child and had invented a realm of the imagination for himself. The book that meant the most to me was *David Copperfield*. In my mind, I took every step in David's odyssey from infancy to manhood, through tragedy and humour, as he gained ever more control over a life that had begun in terrible circumstances. I fell in love with little Emily alongside him. I was sorry when I finished the book — I didn't want to leave David Copperfield's world.

I took to writing poetry, mostly whimsies about streams and lakes, touched with sadness and thoughts of impending disaster. In a poem inspired by thoughts of my father and his cause, I imagined that I would replace him in the great struggle and that he would live on through me:

> Lie down and rest and let me walk,
> for I am strong.
> When I have reached the goal we sought, you
> shall have made it too.

But Oakwood would not go away, however much I might wish it. Once a week all the boys in the school received military instruction. In the gymnasium, we were divided into platoons of about thirty boys each. We marched out onto the floor of the gym, lining up three deep and ten across. Teachers who had been captains, majors and colonels barked out the orders in these exercises, which were part of what was called "citizenship training." We stood at attention or at ease while these former officers relived their glory days and lectured us on the meaning of service, country, empire, queen and manhood. Then we marched. "Attention, right turn, forward march, left wheel..."

Drilling was followed by instructions on how to clean and fire guns. Rifles that had known their best days sometime around the Crimean War were distributed. We were taught how to disassemble one, clean it and put it back together again. Early on in the process, I managed to pull the trigger and release the hammer of the rifle on my finger. My father didn't like the anti-Communism of my school, but he had no problem with the military instruction. Like most veterans, he didn't mind the idea of his sons being introduced to the ways of the armed forces.

The prize for all this training came the day we went downstairs to the shooting range in the school basement. Calling it a shooting range was grandiose; actually, we were firing our rifles down the basement hallway, which had students' lockers on either side. Cardboard targets were hung at the end of the hallway, and our goal, of course, was to hit them. Quite often, shots went wild and tore holes in the lockers and their contents. Students sometimes went home with bullet holes in their jackets and spent cartridges in their pockets. Shooting up the lockers was not an entirely bad thing, because the school basement was overrun with cockroaches. Often when you opened your brown lunch bag and took out your sandwich, you'd see that a small corner of the crust had been eaten. I always thought that in target practice at least we were hitting the odd cockroach.

On Remembrance Day, all of the thousand students at the school gathered to honour the Canadians who had died in the two world wars and in Korea. For our principal, Major Horning, it was the grand occasion of the year. The rest of us stood motionless as a colour guard of students in full military gear marched into the auditorium. The march was slow, sombre, accompanied by muffled drums. The last post was played. My heart went out to the lone student with the bugle. Finally, Principal Horning, a large, ungainly man, stepped up to the podium. The principal was not a gifted public speaker, but his emotion carried him through. He told the tale of his lost comrades who had died in the trenches in France in the First World War. By the end, Major Horning was in tears. He stumbled, hunched and stiff, off the stage.

As winter deepened, the military training at Oakwood intensified. We were working toward the day in June that the school's cadets put on an evening-long display of their talents at the Fort York Armoury in downtown Toronto. At this inspection, a serving major general or general would be brought in to look us over. The inspection was the big annual event for the boys at Oakwood.

We were issued khaki uniforms in January. We had to clean and press them, applying spit and polish to the metal bits and buffing our heavy black shoes to perfection. Our uniforms were constantly checked to make sure they were up to snuff. Students who did not meet the mark were sent to stand in the corner of the gym for an hour. Once, as I stood in my platoon looking more than usually clueless, a teacher-officer inquired deafeningly whether I spoke English. I thought ruefully that my own army, in which I was the general, had been much more agreeable.

The military training at Oakwood dovetailed with the rest of citizenship training, which involved swimming classes and health classes. Mr. Lobb, our teacher for both these classes, was a burly, thuggish-looking man with a balding head and pronounced brows. He looked remarkably like Senator McCarthy. Our health classes with him were coeducational. One time, he passed a human brain around the class for us to touch and feel. In his rather brutish style, he lectured us on the various systems of the body. He told us how blood circulation and breathing worked and explained that these were involuntary activities. They just happened. Then he moved on to the reproductive system, stating with great emphasis that, unlike the other systems, reproduction was entirely voluntary. He was wrought up, even angry as he made his cryptic comments. What went where and why was never explained.

Mr. Lobb spiced up our health classes with lengthy monologues on the virtues of obedience. Sometimes these monologues were carried over into swimming classes, which were not coeducational. The boys swam in the nude in the frigid Oakwood pool. After we had undressed and walked through the shower, Mr. Lobb lined us up around the edge of the pool. We stood naked and shivering while he expounded on society and citizenship. Following that he told us what kind of swimming exercise was expected for the day. By the time we got into the pool, half the class time was over. I was always glad to get my skinny, bare body under the water where it was not quite so visible.

Fainting was the great fear of the boys at Oakwood as the annual military inspection approached. The worry was that standing at attention in the hot, stale air of the armoury could cause you to keel over. I had never fainted in my life, and it had never occurred to me that I might. But the danger of fainting was driven home by Mr. Lobb, who warned us that it would be necessary to use all of our willpower and various wily tricks to avoid it.

To steel us as the great event approached, we were given lectures on the floor of the gym by various teacher-officers. Fear was natural, we were told, but young men had had to face fear in the line of duty many times before. In one pep talk, as we stood at attention, we were told about the ordeal of the men who had fought in the trenches during the First World War. They had had to cower just below ground level with their heavy gear on, waiting miserably until a huge artillery barrage ended. When the order came, they climbed out of the trench and headed across no man's land, straight toward the enemy soldiers who were raking them with machine-gun fire. By comparison, what faced us was child's play. Despite that lesson, I tortured myself with the thought that I might clatter to the floor in front of thousands of people.

When the big night came we assembled in our platoons outside the armoury and were issued our rifles. At last we were ready to march inside. The band struck up and off we went, each platoon falling into the procession at its appointed time. Inside we took up our positions, standing at attention, rifles in place. We faced the officers, who stood on a reviewing platform at the front. Silence fell in the hall, whose upper balcony was filled with parents and the girls from our school. From one side of the armoury a small party of men in uniform entered and proceeded toward the stand. Out of the corner of my eye, I could see the top muckety-muck himself.

Moustachioed, he was dressed in a khaki uniform with plenty of stripes and medals adorning his jacket. The inspection party made its way slowly across the hall and mounted the platform. Its members seemed to be enjoying themselves in a masculine sort of way. They were in no rush. There was much saluting and hand-shaking as the great man was welcomed to the reviewing stand.

Then began the inspection itself. The general, accompanied by officers who included one or two of our teachers in uniform, began to stroll through the ranks. They walked up and down each line in each platoon, occasionally stopping to stare at a particular cadet. Now and then, they talked to one of the cadets before continuing. Off in the corner, I heard a loud clattering sound. I was sure someone had fainted and was now being stared at by all the girls in the school. Gently, I bent my knees and took a deep breath. I looked up into the balcony, where Mr. Lobb was gazing down at us. He nodded his head slightly and raised his hand to give the OK sign. Anti-climactically, the reviewing party passed down the line in front of us without a glance at my comrades or me.

At halftime, the boys filled the balcony and the girls came out onto the floor dressed in blue bloomers. Who could have guessed what they had been learning during our long weeks of preparation for the inspection? Accompanied by loud music and cheerful streamers, they performed in unison in a dance-gymnastic exercise. I was so relieved that the hard part was over I didn't bother to pay attention.

I was having health problems during this time, but they were more odd than dramatic. I was afflicted with endless throat infections and earaches. Unhappily for me, my childhood coincided with the high point of the tonsillectomy industry among ear, nose and throat specialists. My tonsils and adenoids were first removed when I was two. When I was ten, and still getting throat infections, another doctor informed my parents that my tonsils and adenoids had grown back. In the operating room, as the doctor put the anaesthetic mask over my face, the world revolved dizzily, with bright lights spitting at me before the room turned black. When I came to, my throat was incredibly sore. Four years later, the whole saga would be repeated. I was again taken to a doctor who told us that my tonsils had miraculously sprung back, like some hardy perennial, and were doing me great harm. Yet again I was taken to the hospital. That time they knocked me out with a needle, which was much less horrible, but my throat was just as sore afterward.

My first year at Oakwood was a bust. Between constant throat infections and faked illnesses to avoid school, I missed more than fifty days of classes. In the spring, my mother met with my homeroom teacher, and they decided that I should repeat grade nine. Since I'd accelerated through a grade in public school, that meant I would be the same age as most of the other students in my year.

Another military man, Major Bush, was my homeroom teacher for my second try at grade nine. He was a compact, muscular man with a closed but not unattractive face. He exuded force and stood ramrod straight beside his desk. When he wanted to hear from a student, he pointed at him or her with martial directness. The student was required to rise and step clear of the desk, coming to attention. Slouching was a sin. When you answered a question, you had to begin your answer by crisply addressing him as "Major Bush." Major Bush taught English, but I learned more from him about military bearing than about literature. If he had any insights into the books we read, he didn't bother to impart them to us. His specialty was speed-reading, and his staccato campaign to increase the pace of our reading bore a resemblance to Charlie Chaplin's work on the assembly line in *Modern Times*.

Despite all this, things at Oakwood were better that year. I had grown taller, for one thing, not unimportant for someone who had been the shortest person in the class. And the militarists in the school seemed less obnoxious. Maybe I was just getting used to them.

MY FIRST TWO YEARS of high school were a very active time for my parents politically. After the execution of the Rosenbergs, the central focus, especially for my mother, became the ban-the-bomb movement.

I'd sat on my bicycle for much of one awful Saturday in September 1954 when the sun was a smouldering late-summer monster in the sky. Shafts of light suffocated the leaves and branches on the trees. That morning, my mother had sat me down to explain that the Americans had developed a new and terrible weapon, the hydrogen bomb. In the months previous, I had seen pictures of the ruins of Hiroshima and Nagasaki and attended peace meetings where I heard terrifying descriptions of how radiation from an atomic bomb could make you blind, cause your skin to disintegrate and leave you to suffer a slow and horrible death. My parents had taken me to a Communist meeting where I saw an animated film that depicted two neighbours in their backyards who slowly got drawn into a quarrel and began fighting. At first the fighting was not too serious, but it escalated step by step until the two men ended up tearing each other to pieces. The images played through my mind for days.

Perched on my bicycle that afternoon, I pictured the trees melting away and the centre of the city boiling, with a mushroom cloud rising overhead. My mother had told me that the new bomb would simply vaporize you; if you were far enough away from where it hit, you might see it coming for a few seconds and then you would be gone. For weeks following, I would have nightmares about it.

My parents talked constantly about the bomb. For my mother, it was another thing to worry about, to be added to a long list of existing fears: of disease, radiation from a treatment she'd once received, even the ubiquitous house dust. For my father, the fight against the bomb was part of the job. Banning the bomb had become the high-profile issue for Communists.

My father and mother wore themselves out trying to win liberal-minded non-Communists to the cause. As she had for the Rosenbergs, my mother stood on street corners downtown in the afternoons, collecting signatures on a petition. Sometimes she brought me or one of my siblings along, hoping the presence of a young person would soften anti-Communist responses. I hated going. I always tensed when she approached someone for a signature, fearing that we would get a stream of abuse. Often enough, we did.

My father spoke at public meetings on the issue, frequently sharing the platform with clergymen who were not members of the Party. While Communists mounted their campaigns on the goal of peace, the Korean War had given the world a foretaste of what a major conflagration between the West and the Communist powers would be like.

Despite the hatred I often saw for my parents' brand of politics, Communist political campaigns were not without some noteworthy successes. A well-known Communist personality was Joseph (J. B.) Salsberg, who had won a seat in the provincial legislature for the LPP for several consecutive terms. Salsberg had got his start in life as a hat maker, and he rose quickly through the ranks of his local union to become the leader of the Industrial Union of Needle Trades Workers. J. B., as he was usually called, was a large man with protruding eyebrows, a shock of receding reddish hair and a generous moustache. He was a man of huge charm who loved to meet people and talk to them; he always assumed that they would reciprocate by adoring him. He was often a guest in our living room, talking brightly in his rich, powerful voice while nibbling incessantly at some bit of pastry.

J. B. had managed to win the St. Andrew's riding in downtown Toronto in the 1943 provincial election. He held onto the seat in 1945, and then, despite the Cold War and the deep anti-Communism it

engendered, he won two more terms, in 1948 and 1951. The main
street of J. B.'s Toronto was Spadina, where he was king among the
garment workers and was known in every delicatessen along the
wide thoroughfare. His main electoral base was the large Jewish
population who lived in the riding.

The LPP's headquarters in Toronto was a few doors west of
Spadina at 274 College Street — the address I had blurted out to my
grade one teacher. My father worked out of this office, and in 1955 he
managed J. B.'s campaign in the St. Andrew's riding when another
general election was called. My brother and I played a small part in
the campaign, delivering J. B.'s flyers door to door.

The one job I really enjoyed was putting up election posters
for the party on the Christie Street railway bridge. This task my
brother and I carried out under the welcome cover of darkness.
After supper, Gord and I put the posters, along with a hammer and
some short nails with big heads, into a *Toronto Star* delivery bag. It
was two short blocks to the bridge, and once we got there we headed
up the driveway past the Eaton's warehouse that was then located
beside it. From there it was a short climb up the cinders and onto
the railway tracks. The CPR line was busy, so we had to watch out
for moving trains. There were often boxcars sitting on one of the
tracks, too, and you had to take care that an engine wasn't about to
shunt some of them. We played up there a lot, so we were used to
climbing between the cars.

Once on the bridge, we waited until no one was coming down
the street in a car or on foot. Then Gord handed me the hammer
and some nails. I leaned over the bridge rail, straightened out the
poster and nailed it into place. If I heard footsteps, I would finish
the job quickly. Then we would lie back in the shadows, our faces
drenched in sweat.

We would put up two posters on each side of the bridge. A
couple of times we walked along the rail line west to Shaw Street

and east to Bathurst Street to put up posters on those bridges as well. One night, we were startled when a man leapt out of the shadows and stood right in front of us. "What are you kids doing here? I bet you're the ones who broke the windows at Silverwoods," he snarled. Silverwoods was a big dairy on Dupont Street, whose premises backed onto the railway tracks. Gord and I had evidently come upon a company security guard. To demonstrate our innocence, I pulled an election sign out of the delivery bag and showed it to him. Once he saw that we were putting up signs for the LPP, he had no further interest in us. He was preoccupied with vandals, not Communists.

Though we postered in other spots from time to time, our main goal in the sign campaign was to "hold the bridge" on Christie Street. Whenever someone tore our posters down, we went out and put up new ones. The beauty of the operation was that it was secretive. You could exult when you walked under the signs in daylight, but no one would ever know who had done the dirty work.

In addition to these furtive nighttime operations, I participated in the street theatre that was a part of Salsberg's campaign. Often I sat in the sound car that cruised up and down residential streets, blaring out the message of where and when the candidate would speak to the people. The car was festooned with large posters and pictures of J. B. And the sound system was awful — the music it produced was loud and scratchy, and the voice was hard to understand. Why people put up with this cacophonous invasion of their neighbourhoods I don't know, but all of the parties used sound cars in those days. I liked riding in the car. Even though I was not many blocks from my house, I didn't worry that my friends or neighbours would see me. It was much safer to be there than on the street with my mother collecting signatures.

A favourite spot for a rally was the street corner in front of the LPP headquarters. Crowds would gather at the appointed time, and my father would climb out of the sound car, mike in hand. J. B., clearly in his element, embraced the mike and made love to the crowd with his full, round voice. No matter what he talked about — the housing shortage, the cost of living — he held his listeners in the palm of his hand. After his oration, J. B. dove into the crowd, greeting people and shaking hands, a real celebrity.

The 1955 campaign was a hard-fought, even bitter, contest between Salsberg and his main challenger, Allan Grossman, the Progressive Conservative candidate. In the end, Grossman won, and J. B.'s stint in the Ontario legislature came to an end. Not long afterward, a federal by-election was called in the riding that contained Salsberg's old provincial constituency. Salsberg ran and lost again. His days in electoral politics were over. And the winds of change were blowing for the Party, as we would soon see.

Thirteen

ESCAPE FROM A SPIRITUAL GULAG

ONE SATURDAY NIGHT in the winter of 1956, I was watching the Dorsey brothers' television show with my parents. It was a weekly show that featured Jimmy and Tommy Dorsey and their swing-band music. Pretty boring stuff, I thought. But then something unexpected happened. Out onto the stage came a long-haired, guitar-playing singer named Elvis Presley. It was the King's first appearance on a national broadcast, and for me it was electric. I'd never heard of rock 'n' roll, but I was an instant convert. My parents watched in a mood of mirthful incomprehension. We were a strange family in many ways, but on this night we reacted the same way as millions of other families across the continent, with enraptured kids on one side and puzzled parents on the other. And although we couldn't know it then, our lives were about to undergo a fundamental change, a transformation that I would never have dared contemplate. The pillar that had defined my existence from the moment of my birth was about to crumble.

A dream came true for my father in January of that year. The top Party brass in Canada arranged for him to visit the Soviet Union to tour factories, hospitals and schools in the late spring. At last he would observe Soviet accomplishments first-hand. As a special reward for his two decades of devotion to the cause, he would be sent to a luxury spa on the Black Sea for an assessment of his health and a course of treatment to cure whatever ailed him. The idea was that he would thereby be reinvigorated and return home to carry on the struggle with fervour.

The weeks before he left, during which I had my third tonsillectomy, were sad. My father was going to be away for more than three months. But the whole family shared in his excitement as he prepared for his trip by immersing himself in the study of basic Russian. He passed his hours in the living room surrounded by stacks of papers, books and primers. As always when he lounged in his armchair, working this way, he piled his favourite long-play recordings of Beethoven and Tchaikovsky on the record player. He toiled with the music blaring, munching his way through a plate of sandwiches at his side.

After his departure, we returned to our normal routines. The ice rink in the park at Christie and Davenport was in excellent shape that winter, and I played hockey almost every afternoon, not returning home until after dark. My father sent frequent letters during his absence, but his tales of Moscow and other parts of the Soviet Union seemed distant. Not until his return would we hear his stories in full. And by then, the world Communist movement would be living in an entirely different epoch.

As the date of my father's return grew closer, we arranged to meet him in Montreal. It would be a great time, seeing him again and doing the rounds of our relatives there. I could hardly wait to board the train with my mother and Gord and Linda. But on June 5, a bombshell fell on Communists the world over. The *New York Times* published what it claimed was the complete text of the address by Nikita Khrushchev, General Secretary of the Communist Party of the Soviet Union, to a closed session of the twentieth congress of the Party. In this explosive address, which had been delivered in

Moscow in February, Khrushchev acknowledged—the first time a top Soviet Communist had ever done so—that serious crimes had been committed while Stalin was in power.

In the months prior to the *New York Times* story, there had been rumblings in the press that alerted the world's Communists something big was going on. My father had arrived in the Soviet Union at about the time the twentieth congress was beginning its sessions, but the critical session was closed to party officials at his level. Uncle Jack picked us up in a taxi at the railway station in Montreal and took us to his house. It was in our days there, while we awaited my father's arrival, that we learned the news of Khrushchev's speech. The *New York Times*'s reprint of the speech's full text prompted banner headlines in newspapers around the world.

My father was scheduled to fly from Leningrad to Helsinki, and from there to London. As he would later recount, he found a British newspaper that blared the shocking news of Khrushchev's speech at a kiosk in the Helsinki airport. Unbeknownst to him, all the time he had been meeting Soviet students and visiting factories, the leadership of his Party had been discussing the crimes of Stalin. The Soviet people had been kept in the dark, just as he had been. As he flew west reading the cataclysmic news, massive doubts were sprouting about the Party. His life, and those of many others, would never be the same.

When my father was back with us, he was immediately flung into a round of gatherings with dozens of relatives jammed into small spaces eating, smoking, drinking and talking. It was a never-ending bazaar, shifting from one aunt's house to another. Changes in scene were announced breathlessly on the telephone by Aunt Dora, who would phone the others to announce "They're here," then hang up without another word to dial the next relative. Naturally my father was the guest of honour, and rooms fell silent when he spoke of his trip. He started in, as he always did, with a shaggy dog–style approach to the subject. He told stories about arriving in Moscow, about seeing the city, about going to the ballet. He had stayed in one of Moscow's finest hotels. In the mornings, local Communist officials took him to city schools, where polite, neatly dressed students greeted him. They impressed him with their foreign-language skills as they read aloud passages from authors such as the American adventure writer Jack London. London, a stark realist in his prose, had always received the stamp of approval from Soviet authorities.

The majority of Soviet doctors were women. My father liked that, although it crossed his mind that this might mean the profession had a lower status. Women also did physical jobs like street-cleaning and garbage collection. That, too, my father liked. Here was more evidence of the equality of women in a socialist country.

But he was stunned at how poor the country looked. As he travelled around Moscow and other cities, he saw many shabby buildings and poorly dressed people. Soviet Russia was much less developed than he had imagined. The officials who accompanied him prattled on about the rapid construction of new apartment units. But right before his eyes was the unadorned evidence of crummy cinderblock edifices thrown up during the Stalin era. He was horrified, and he told us more than once that the doors in these buildings were not properly hung and the windows didn't fit. As my father walked un-shepherded along the streets of Moscow, he ran into black marketeers who wore loose-fitting garments to conceal valuables, often watches. They came up to him surreptitiously, trying to make a sale in return for Western currency. He described the lugubrious process by which they would reach up their sleeves and slyly take down some enticing item.

But all was not dispiriting in the Soviet Union, my father told the assembled group. He went frequently to the Bolshoi Ballet to see *Swan Lake* and other favourites. In the theatre, he spotted top members of the Soviet party establishment ensconced in the best boxes. And there were Party receptions with pots of the finest caviar and plenty of vodka to wash it down. It was a heady experience to go from being a member of a marginal, reviled organization in Canada to being feted by the Soviet establishment, as though one actually represented the working class of one's country. No wonder Communist leaders from the West looked forward to their trips to the motherland.

Members of the Party hierarchy, whether they were Soviet or foreign Communists, were never allowed to forget their rank. Tim Buck, the leader of Canada's Communists, was in Moscow at the same time as my father. But unlike my father, Buck was present to hear Khrushchev's crucial closed-session address.

Even at his own level in the hierarchy, my father was sharply reminded that he too had responsibilities. He had travelled to the Soviet Union with a fellow Communist from Saskatchewan, who ranked lower in the Party than my father did. The Saskatchewan comrade was of Ukrainian origin, and he was excited about the chance to visit a part of the Ukraine where much of his family still lived. One day, a shadowy fellow approached my father. The stranger, who identified himself as an official in the Party, informed my father rather roughly that there were some suspicions about his colleague from Western Canada. Members of the man's family had been arrested and sent to camps in Siberia for political crimes. The Party official asked my father if he would go with his Canadian comrade to the Ukraine to keep a close eye on him.

This was an unpleasant idea, my father thought. He reckoned that his colleague would be disappointed to return to his relatives in the company of someone who outranked him and would therefore be accorded the top status at local receptions. For this reason, he turned down the request.

My father had considered paying a visit to the region where his own mother and father were born. But so much had changed since Freda and Getzel had set out for North America. When my father's parents left their home in Bukovina at the beginning of the twentieth century, the territory was in the eastern portion of the Austro-Hungarian Empire. In 1941, the Romanian army had slaughtered all of the Jews who remained in Bukovina when it invaded the region as participants in Hitler's assault on the Soviet Union. Relatives who lived in Romania itself, where most Jews survived the war, eventually found their way to the land that became Israel. In the end, my father decided not to visit Bukovina, where the traces of his parents' origins had been so thoroughly trampled.

At the health resort on the Black Sea, which was reserved for top Party officials, my father spent several weeks having his health monitored by doctors and nurses and following a daily regime they had prescribed. It was a rather dotty place, with theories about health that were hard to fathom. During the first week, huge doses of sleep were emphasized. With the aid of drugs, my father told us, he slept most of the time. Why the sleeping, why the drugs? I have never been able to figure it out. After his long sleep came lengthy walks and fresh air in a terrain of hills and trees. This solitary exercise was followed by social activities such as volleyball — always a favourite sport among Communists, since it emphasized teamwork and cooperation as well as competition.

At any other time, my father's relatives would have loved these long-winded tales. But on everyone's mind this visit was Khrushchev's speech and what my father thought about it. Reminiscences about workers in factories were well and good, but were the accusations being made about Stalin true? Uncle Jack, because of the time he spent in a Canadian internment camp during the war, was especially stern in wanting answers.

My own mind was in a whirr. In the continuing crush of family gatherings, I hardly had an opportunity to speak to my father alone. But I could feel the foundations of my life buckling. I had been taught that the Russian Revolution was the most far-reaching and progressive event in human history. All my life Stalin had been the peerless leader, followed without question and revered in death. Suddenly the vocabulary was changing, and with all the deep conservatism of youth, I found it immensely disturbing. "Cult of leadership" was the queer, elliptical new phrase on people's lips. At our family fetes, everyone was talking about it.

If my father was experiencing deep turmoil about Khrushchev's speech, he didn't show it. He had converted some of his relatives to Communism, and it was up to him to provide a compass in this time of rising confusion. He remained what he had always been: an optimist showing others the way ahead. He explained to the assembled group that Stalin had gone too far. The great leader had become too much of a one-man show, towering over the rest of the Party and the Communist world. A personality cult was a bad thing. It went to a leader's head and could influence him to do terrible things. At first, this cult of personality idea didn't sound like such a big deal to me. Stalin had been a wonderful person who had led his people through perilous times. Why not allow him a little glory? I thought. Could that be such a bad thing?

A few weeks later, back in Toronto, my father took me to the screening of a Soviet film on the Russian war against Nazi Germany. In the last segment of the film, after excruciating scenes depicting the Russian assault on Berlin in the spring of 1945, a Russian soldier cuts down the swastika and hoists the hammer and sickle over the rubble of Hitler's chancellery. The film ends with a tribute to Stalin. The great leader's aircraft lands, and he emerges from it smiling. He is shot from below to enhance his magnificence as he acknowledges the cheers of the adoring crowd.

This final scene provoked much tsk-tsking from the pro-Party audience, and my father was among those shaking their heads. There it was again, Stalin indulging in the cult of personality. But to me it appeared that an essentially good man had been guilty of breaking a few house rules, taking too many encores at public ceremonies. Again, I wondered why the reaction among Communists was so strong.

At the house on Melita Street, meetings were held night after night. Sometimes, before they began, I sat in on discussions involving small groups of my parents' cronies. By now, the criticism of Stalin was being extended to Canada's Communist leader, Tim Buck. No longer affectionately called Tim, he was now referred to as "the Old Man." Repeatedly, I heard the Old Man being scorned. He was a hard-liner, people said, a Moscow-liner. They accused him of simply going along with Khrushchev and the Soviet Party, an accusation I found puzzling.

I felt a nagging loyalty to Tim Buck. I had always been taught how brave he was, how he had gone to jail in the thirties in the fight for workers' rights. Now Party members were turning on him. Besides, I couldn't follow the logic. If Khrushchev was right in his criticisms of Stalin, then why were they mad at Tim Buck for following the Moscow line? Here were people who had followed the Moscow line themselves, through thick and thin, and yet now they seemed to think it a matter of principle to stand up to Moscow. I told my father and his friends that it bothered me to hear them call Tim Buck the Old Man. Some of them looked at me blankly. Others smiled, amused at a teenager's response to the crisis in their lives. If they had bothered to pay real attention to me, they would have seen a caricature of themselves. I was, after all, their creation. But they were in no mood to consider that.

The truth was that the critics of Tim Buck among Canadian Communists were in deep denial. Given the horrific truth, Khrushchev had presented an airbrushed, whitewashed criticism of the Stalin years. His speech amounted to a virtual apology for Stalin. Much time would pass before I realized how deeply offensive it was to use the phrase "cult of personality" to describe one of the

worst mass murderers in history. But when people have been participants in a foul undertaking, and have put it at the centre of their
lives, their first steps back are bound to be awkward ones.

Canadian Communists had been particularly orthodox in their
loyalty to Moscow at key moments. But one prominent figure in the
Party had been taking a more independent course. J. B. Salsberg
had crossed swords with Tim Buck a number of times over the
decades. In the early fifties, Salsberg had become increasingly concerned by reports he was receiving of widespread anti-Semitism
in the Soviet Union. In 1952, he made it known to the leadership
of the Canadian party that he believed anti-Semitism was rife in
the socialist motherland. Pressure was exerted on him to withdraw
these charges, but he refused to back down, and he was subse-
quently removed from the Party's national executive.

Indeed, my father had had his own significant moment of dis-
sidence within the Party before the great meltdown that followed
Khrushchev's revelations. Two years earlier, he had presented a
lengthy paper arguing that the LPP should make the struggle for
Canadian independence the centrepiece of its orientation. Although
he was not demoted from the Central Committee as a consequence,
his paper was rejected as a display of bourgeois nationalism. Over
the preceding quarter century, there had been a number of debates
about whether it was correct for Canadian Communists to advocate
the independence of Canada from the United States. In 1929, Tim
Buck had himself been denounced by Moscow for putting too much
emphasis on the issue. At first Buck had tried to defend his position.
Later, he backed down and admitted the error of his ways. By the
1950s, the pendulum within the LPP had swung again, and Canadian
Communists declared their opposition to having Canada reduced to
the status of a colony producing raw materials for the U.S.

The debate about Stalinism began among the Party's top leaders just weeks after the twentieth congress ended in February. Even

though the full text of Khrushchev's speech would not be available for months to come, early leaks in the press indicated that Stalin's leadership had come under unprecedented attack. J. B. Salsberg's independence and his popularity in the Jewish community placed him in a pivotal position as the great debate unfolded. For a time, the fate of Canadian Communism seemed to hang in the balance. Perhaps the forces around Salsberg would overturn the old leadership, and those who were genuinely independent of Moscow would seize control of the Party. My father supported Salsberg's side in the struggle, and he devoted himself to it until it became clear that Tim Buck and the hard-liners were going to win in the end.

The debate within the Party had been underway for a few months when another event in the Soviet sphere of Europe shocked the world. In November 1956, Soviet aircraft bombed Budapest, and Red Army tanks rolled into the city to suppress the anti-Stalinist revolution of the Hungarian people. In the weeks that followed, Hungarians came out into the streets to face Soviet tanks, often with only their bare hands, and the world saw what, for a time, appeared to be the liberation of the country. In the end, three thousand Soviet tanks decided the issue. Thousands of Hungarians died during the suppression of the revolution and the reign of terror that followed. Among their number was Hungarian Prime Minister Imre Nagy, a reform Communist who had brought non-Communists into his government in the last desperate days and had announced the withdrawal of his country from the Warsaw Pact. Nagy was executed by a Soviet firing squad following a secret trial and buried in a pauper's grave.

As the Khrushchev regime bloodied the streets of Budapest, Communist loyalists were further shaken. Some had clung to the hope that, with his condemnation of Stalin, Khrushchev was placing the Soviet Union on a new non-repressive course. Hardliners concocted the theory that the Hungarian revolution was a reactionary betrayal of socialism engineered by the Americans. But those who were shocked by what they had learned of Stalinism were appalled by what they saw in Hungary. Newsreels of Soviet tanks running down unarmed men and women put paid to the idea that the Soviet Union's Eastern European allies were free and happy peoples living in a voluntary alliance with Moscow. For tens of thousands who had devoted their lives to the struggle, it was a bitter betrayal. For many Communists around the world, Hungary was the last straw.

The acrimony in the Canadian party went on for months. By the spring of 1957, nearly half the members of the national executive and hundreds of rank and file members had left the Party. Most of my father's closest friends quit the organization.

More months would pass before my parents made their own momentous decision. Then one evening, they called my brother and sister and me together and sat us down in the living room. "We are leaving the Party," my father announced sombrely. "We're going to do it very quietly. There will be no formal resignation."

So there it was. There wasn't much fight in my father that day. That had been beaten out of him through the long agony that followed Khrushchev's revelations and the invasion of Hungary. For years, my father and mother had devoted themselves completely to a cause that had now been exposed as hollow, as evil. My siblings and I had nothing to say.

Fourteen

AFTERWORD

MY PARENTS STUCK TENACIOUSLY to their exit strategy for leaving the Party. Old friendships were quietly dropped, in most cases never to be resumed. For some of the people who went through the same wrenching change, my parents' approach was inexplicable. How could they simply walk away from it all, dropping the past as though it had never existed? Invitations to meetings were ignored. On a few occasions, my mother encountered former close friends who couldn't understand why the Laxers were being so unfriendly. My father, who had thrown over the religion of his father three decades earlier, was now turning his back on the Party that had been his life for over twenty years. The cloak of secrecy once extended over our family's Communist activities was now used to shroud its Communist past.

My father applied himself with characteristic single-mindedness to the new task ahead. When the Party income stopped, my mother began to work again as a social worker, first part-time, then full-time. My father tried his hand at being a bookkeeper, then made the decision to go back to graduate school. He obtained another M.A. in psychology. While working as a psychologist at the city's main psychiatric hospital on Queen Street, and later at Toronto General Hospital, he pushed on with his studies, completing his Ph.D. in the early 1960s. He took a post teaching psychology at the newly founded York University, and that was followed by an appointment at the Ontario Institute for Studies in Education.

When he left the Party in 1956, more than half my father's life still stretched before him. With his usual energy and optimism, he devoted himself to new projects. For the first fifteen years, his main efforts revolved around his studies and his clinical and academic work. As the 1970s began, though, he returned increasingly to the great love of his life, politics and the struggle for social justice. By then, a new generation had transformed the Left in Europe and North America. The New Left had nearly toppled the government of Charles de Gaulle in France in 1968. It was challenging the postwar order in West Germany, and its adherents were marching for nuclear disarmament in Britain. In the United States, the young had thrown themselves into the struggle for civil rights and the movement to end the war in Vietnam. In Canada, the youthful Left participated in anti-war campaigns and poured its energies into the Quebecois struggle for self-determination and the battle against American corporate control.

My father was inspired to join the fray. For the next quarter of a century, he threw himself into the battles among the social democrats and Liberals and fought to Canadianize the petroleum industry. He became interested in liberation theology, environmentalism and feminism. He helped found the Council of Canadians and wrote books, most notably one on the trade union movement of the 1970s. He and I co-authored a book on Canadian politics in 1977.

As the years passed, I pieced together the history of the Communist Party, whose traumatic story had been only partially passed on to me during my young years. The crucial missing chapter concerned the signing of the Nazi-Soviet Pact in August 1939 and its momentous aftermath.

I knew the Communists had struggled against the appeasers in the 1930s. What I had not been told was that, in the months following Munich, the British and the French stiffened their spines against appeasement. The following March, when Hitler occupied the rump of Czechoslovakia, the Chamberlain government warned that Britain would guarantee the territorial integrity of other states that stood in Hitler's path. For the next few months, the Western powers and the Soviet Union carried on negotiations to forge an alliance against Nazi Germany. The alliance was to go into effect if Hitler invaded Poland. But the alliance between the West and the Soviet Union was never consummated.

Instead of an alliance between the Soviet Union and the West, a diplomatic revolution occurred as a result of a startling initiative from Berlin. On August 22, 1939, the world was stunned by the news that the two implacable ideological foes, Nazi Germany and Soviet Russia, had signed a non-aggression pact. Not only did Hitler and Stalin agree not to oppose one another, they made a sweeping deal to divide Eastern Europe between them. Germany would invade Poland and occupy most of the country, up to an agreed line east of Warsaw. East of that line was the territory the Soviet Union was to occupy. For their part, the Soviets would be allowed to occupy the Baltic republics of Latvia, Lithuania and Estonia. In addition, they could seize strategically important territory in Finland and Romania.

I was an adult before I realized that the Hitler-Stalin Pact opened the door for the outbreak of the Second World War. At dawn on September 1, Hitler launched his blitzkrieg offensive against Poland. Two days later, Britain and France declared war on Germany. Following a parliamentary debate, Canada declared war on September 10. The United States held out until Japan attacked Pearl Harbor on December 7, 1941.

Communists in the Western democracies found themselves in a predicament they would not have thought possible only a few weeks earlier. My father's world was turned upside down. The three-way poker game of the thirties had not ended as Communists in the Western world had feared, with the Nazis fighting the Soviets while the West stayed off to the side. Instead, the West was at war with Hitler, and it was Stalin who was standing on the sidelines. These developments left the world's Communists in disarray. The first instinct of the French, British and Canadian Communist parties was to endorse the war efforts of their countries. But on September 18, 1939, Stalin issued a directive to all Communist parties, ordering them not to support the war against Hitler. In his directive, the supreme leader of the world's Communists proclaimed, "The present war is an imperialist and unjust war for which the bourgeoisie of all the belligerent States bear equal responsibility. In no country can the Communist Parties or the working class support the war. The bourgeoisie is not conducting the war against fascism as Chamberlain and the leaders of the Labour Party pretend. War is carried on between two groups of imperialist countries for world domination."

By the end of September, every Communist party in the world had adopted the line laid down by Stalin. While in a few cases there were some dissidents who refused to go along with the new orthodoxy, the Communist Party of Canada went over to Stalin's position without dissent. The U.S. Communist Party was even quicker in its conversion, adopting the new Stalin line on the basis of a broadcast from Moscow that predated the leader's directive by a few days. Shockingly, Communists in Canada, who had spent years complaining that the social democrats were not standing up to Hitler, now condemned them for their treachery in backing the war against him.

After the fall of Poland, the so-called "phony war" got underway. During these months of apparent non-conflict, the Communist Party remained legal in Canada, and Canadian Communists denounced the war. During the wartime federal election, in March

1940, the Communist Party of Canada campaigned for Canada's withdrawal from the conflict. The party's election manifesto included this message: "In this war the Canadian capitalists plan to revel in luxury at home, raking in the mounting piles of profits, while sending our sons to rot and die in the trenches of someone else on a far-off continent." Far from being in the vanguard of the struggle against Hitler, Communists became the allies of others who wanted to stay out of the war. The Party was outlawed by the Canadian government in June of that year.

During our many discussions as I was growing up, my father proudly told me about the things Communists had achieved over the years. What he *didn't* tell me was that Communists, at Stalin's behest, had undermined their countries' war efforts against Hitler. Instead, his explanation was that Stalin had figured out he couldn't trust the West, and he needed precious time to build up the Soviet military to be ready for the coming war with Germany. It was Stalin's shrewd calculation, my father insisted, that had saved the Soviet Union.

Much later, reading on my own, I was stunned to learn that in that dark hour, in the spring of 1940 when France fell, and Canada next to Britain was the most important country in the war against Hitler, Canadian Communists had wanted to halt the fighting. It took me a long time to work my way through the convoluted explanation my father had given me about the Communists and the war. I believe the tellers of false tales are almost as damaged by them as the hearers are, and I wonder if, by peddling that story to me, my father managed to keep the distortions alive in his own mind. When, as an adult, I told my him that I could never comprehend his going along with the Nazi–Soviet Pact, he didn't argue. He knew by then there was no point in trying to defend the indefensible.

After the Nazi invasion of the Soviet Union on June 22, 1941, Communists became stalwart advocates of the war effort, completely reversing their previous stand. In January 1943, the Canadian party's Central Committee hashed out the issue at a meeting in Toronto. The battle lines were drawn up not over whether the anti-war position had been correct but over which anti-war position was correct. Tim Buck, along with a couple of associates, had fled across the border to hide out in New York City when the Party was pronounced an illegal organization. Once back in Canada, although the Party was still technically illegal, Buck and his supporters took on the leaders who had stayed in the country while the police were rounding up Party members. The Buck line on the war, before the invasion of the Soviet Union, had been "Withdraw Canada from the Imperialist War," whereas the line of the underground leaders had been "Withdraw Canada from the British Empire." Buck's side prevailed, and the losing side had to grovel and confess its errors. Leslie Morris, one of the losers, vowed to overcome "the pervasion of petty bourgeois nonsense into my political opinions and work... I must value more decisively and more politically the leadership and opinions of comrade Buck, and recognize, as I failed to do, his political authority and maturity." Crow was always a favourite dish at such events.

Why did my father fall for the Communist Party line for so long? What stopped him from clueing in to the horrors of Stalinism, already being written about with considerable acuity by the late 1930s? How could my father, whose very reason for becoming active in politics was to fight Hitler, have stomached the Nazi–Soviet Pact and the Party's initial opposition to Canada's participation in the war?

Part of the answer lies in the circumstances of the times. Western countries were far from faultless during the years my father was a Communist. There was the appeasement of Nazi Germany by the British and the French governments before the war. Afterward, there were the Cold War persecutions of Communists and others on the Left in the United States, Canada and other Western countries.

From the thirties to the fifties, workers in North America and Western Europe were brutally repressed as they fought for higher wages and better working conditions. There were highly publicized interventions by the United States that successfully overthrew legally established governments such as the Mossadegh government in Iran in 1953 and the government of Guatemala in 1954. For my father, these outrageous wrongs continually rekindled his faith.

But no listing of the grave shortcomings of Western countries can ever excuse his blind adherence to Stalinism. There is no equivalency here. One could oppose social injustice and political repression in the West and CIA crimes throughout the world without supporting Stalin's regime and without adhering to the Moscow line in one's political activities. Attempts to explain away adherence to Stalinism just don't work. I will not, I cannot forget the moment when my father told me about Stalin's death. It is an obscenity with which I still have to live. Yet my generation has been much less susceptible than my father's to the lure of totalitarian leaders. And not only did we not have to fight a war against the Nazis, we became much better off materially than those who went before. If I had been my father's age, would I have made the same mistakes? Honestly, I have to say I don't know.

The first decades of the twentieth century were a time when millions of people were drawn to Communist plans to remake the world. The "new man" who was to bestride the planet became the excuse for horrendous crimes. My youthful instincts about him had been accurate. In some ways, the new man was a horrific creation of nineteenth-century science, with its iron rules and determinism gone mad. The new man was a Frankenstein's monster.

The year after my parents left the Party, we moved out of the old house on Melita Street and into a house in North Toronto. I switched from Oakwood to North Toronto Collegiate, where the annual military inspection was a joke during which we stood in white shirts and whispered rude lyrics — Hitler he only had one ball, Goering had two but they were small, Himmler had something similar, but Dr. Goebbels had no balls at all" — while the band played "Colonel Bogy." It would be years before I could talk about some parts of what I had been through, decades before I would talk about the rest. But right after we moved to North Toronto, I got my real birthday back. And I started to tell people what my father actually did for a living.

In those first wonderful months after my parents left the Party, I was like an immigrant in my own land, seeing it, feeling it with deep intensity, and knowing that it was mine. In another respect, all I felt had always been inside me. I was home.

Sometimes I drive to Melita Street to look at the old neighbourhood. It seems much smaller now than when it was the centre of my world. But if I stay long enough, the old feelings come back, and I can imagine my mother and father walking down Melita arm in arm, on their way to the narrow, three-storey house at number 226.

My mother and father in my maternal grandparents' garden.

TOP LEFT: *With my father before he was sent overseas.*
BOTTOM LEFT: *With my mother and Gord.*
ABOVE: *With my mother and father, 1943.*

TOP: *My father after the war.* BOTTOM: *With my father, mother, maternal grand-father and grandmother, Aunt Margaret and Uncle Peter, 1943.* TOP RIGHT: *My paternal grandfather and grandmother with their children and my grandfather's mother, circa 1911. Seated, left to right: Baba Sarah with Rebecca, Getzel, Dora, Freda. Standing, left to right: Malca, Esther, Max, Elsie.* BOTTOM RIGHT: *My father with relatives and friends at his graduation from McGill University, 1937.*

TOP LEFT: *My father and his brother, Max, with their sisters (left to right) Esther, Rebecca, Elsie, Dora, Lily and Malca, circa 1957.* BOTTOM LEFT: *Spouses Dora Laxer, Edna May Laxer and (left to right) Sam Gold, Louis Winkler, Harry Darabaner, Benny Levine and Louis Bernstein, circa 1957.* TOP: *With my father and mother and Gord on Lake Rousseau.* BOTTOM: *With Linda and Gord, 1952.*

At a Communist picnic with my family, 1950.

Acknowledgements

Without the encouragement and active collaboration of a number of people, I could never have written this book.

I am indebted to the following people who read one or more drafts of the manuscript: Gerald Caplan, Ethan Poskanzer, Alisa Poskanzer, Judy Niesenholt, Naomi Duguid, Cathy Lace, Daphne Intrator, Cathy Yolles and John Hutcheson.

Everyone at Douglas & McIntyre has been helpful. In particular, Patsy Aldana believed in this project from the start, giving me indispensable support, both as a dear friend and as a publisher. Barbara Pulling did a wonderful job critiquing, helping shape, and editing the book. Thanks to Pam Robertson for the fine copy-edit. And Jackie Kaiser, my literary agent, was there to push the book along, as always.

My sister Linda and my brother Gord have been unstintingly generous in offering me many hours of their time, during which they pored over every line in the manuscript and ransacked their memories for recollections of days we shared decades ago. I am much indebted to my aunt and uncle Lily and Louis Bernstein, for their assistance in providing family photographs. Aunt Lily's publication *The Lazer Saga* was invaluable.

189

Sandy, my spouse, read various drafts, made suggestions and participated in endless discussions of the book's content.

Grateful as I am to all these people, I alone am responsible for what appears in these pages.

Two books I found very useful in researching this memoir are Norman Penner's *Canadian Communism: The Stalin Years and Beyond* (Toronto: Methuen, 1988) and Robert A. Caro's *Master of the Senate: The Years of Lyndon Johnson, Volume III* (New York: Alfred A. Knopf, 2002). Frank Clarke's article 'Keep Communism Out of Our Schools': Cold War Anti-Communism at the Toronto Board of Education, 1948–1951" (*Labour/Le Travail,* Spring 2002; <http://www. historycooperative.org/journals/llt/49/04clarke.html>) also provided me with additional details from the time, as did the historical components of the CBC's Web site (<http://www.cbc.ca>).

JAMES LAXER (1941–2018) was the award-winning author of more than twenty-five books, including *Staking Claims to a Continent*; the #1 national bestseller *Tecumseh & Brock: The War of 1812*; *Stalking an Elephant: My Discovery of America* (published by the New Press in the United States as *Discovering America*); and *The Border: Canada, the U.S., and Dispatches from the 49th Parallel*. He was a professor of political science in the Department of Equity Studies at York University.

LIST

The A List

The Outlander Gil Adamson
The Circle Game Margaret Atwood
Power Politics Margaret Atwood
Second Words Margaret Atwood
Survival Margaret Atwood
These Festive Nights Marie-Claire Blais
La Guerre Trilogy Roch Carrier
The Hockey Sweater and Other Stories Roch Carrier
Hard Core Logo Nick Craine
Great Expectations Edited by Dede Crane and Lisa Moore
Queen Rat Lynn Crosbie
The Honeyman Festival Marian Engel
The Bush Garden Northrop Frye
Eleven Canadian Novelists Interviewed by Graeme Gibson
Five Legs Graeme Gibson
Death Goes Better with Coca-Cola Dave Godfrey
Technology and Empire George Grant
De Niro's Game Rawi Hage
Kamouraska Anne Hébert
Ticknor Sheila Heti
Waterloo Express Paulette Jiles
No Pain Like This Body Harold Sonny Ladoo
Civil Elegies Dennis Lee
Mermaids and Ikons Gwendolyn MacEwen
Ana Historic Daphne Marlatt
Like This Leo McKay Jr.
Selected Short Fiction of Lisa Moore
Furious Erín Moure
Selected Poems Alden Nowlan
Poems for All the Annettes Al Purdy
Manual for Draft-Age Immigrants to Canada Mark Satin
The Little Girl Who Was Too Fond of Matches Gaétan Soucy
Stilt Jack John Thompson
Made for Happiness Jean Vanier
Basic Black with Pearls Helen Weinzweig
Passing Ceremony Helen Weinzweig
The Big Why Michael Winter
This All Happened Michael Winter

Featuring a new introduction by Mel Watkins

Originally published in 2004, *Red Diaper Baby* is James Laxer's compelling and extraordinary memoir of growing up in a Communist family during the height of the Cold War. When James was born in a Montreal hospital, his father was living in hiding under an assumed name. And when it came time to begin school in Ottawa, James was enrolled under a false birth date. Throughout his childhood he was repeatedly instructed not to tell anyone what his father did for work.

Laxer's parents were dedicated members of the Communist Party, true believers in an ideology that was generally reviled and had been outlawed during much of the Second World War. From an early age, Laxer was collecting signatures on ban-the-bomb petitions, delivering Party flyers door to door, attending the eccentric left-wing Camp Naivelt, and campaigning for the charismatic J. B. Salsberg, a Communist MPP in the Ontario legislature.

Dramatic, humorous, and full of period detail, *Red Diaper Baby* offers a rare look at the McCarthy years through the eyes of a child. It also explains a great deal about Laxer's eventual and crucial role in the founding of the Waffle faction of the NDP, his continued engagement with the left, and his evolution into one of Canada's preeminent intellectuals.

"One of the most gripping and chilling autobiographical accounts ever penned by a Canadian political figure."
— *Ottawa Citizen*

"A rare glimpse into the tiny and now mostly forgotten milieu of Canadian Stalinism." — *National Post*

ANANSI
www.houseofanansi.com
Also available as an ebook

Series design: Brian Morgan
Cover illustration: Patrick Gray

$16.95

ISBN: 978-1-4870-0676-1